Shepherd Crook: BRAZIL

INTRODUCTION TO COMPUTER GRAPHICS STORY WORKBOOK

DYSHANN ANDERSON BFA MDES

innovativeink
PUBLISHING

Publication design, cover image, illustrations, and written by Dyshann Anderson.

Send all inquiries to:
INNOVATIVE INK PUBLISHING
4050 Westmark Drive
Dubuque, IA 52004-1840
www.innovativeinkpublishing.com

ISBN: 9-798-7657-4314-0

ShepherdCrook.com books may be purchased for educational, business, or sales promotional use. For information on panel discussions, lectures, and speaking engagements please write to: Special Markets Department via mail or email, Dyshann.com Hartford, CT, 06103.

Dyshann Anderson, BFA, Savannah College of Art & Design, Information Design, Central Connecticut State University, MDES.

First Shepherd Crook edition published in the United States of America, 2023.

innovativeink
PUBLISHING

SHEPHERD CROOK: RIO DE JANERIO, BRAZIL

INTRODUCTION TO

COMPUTER GRAPHICS

DYSHANN ANDERSON BFA MDES

“A prancha que me
inspira da terra da
criatividade”

“The board that
inspires me
from the land of
creativity”

— Dyshann Anderson

MATERIALS NEEDED

Tools: Graph Paper, Graphic Arts Ruler, Pencils

Software: Adobe Photoshop CC, Illustrator CC, Microsoft Word

Books: Adobe Photoshop CC Classroom in a Book 2022, *Author: Conrad Chavez*. Illustrator CC Classroom in a Book 2022, *Author: Brian Wood*. You are expected to read from this book regularly following the chapters. Seek out the keywords.

Course Description/Course Objectives: This foundational course is an introduction to creating digital art using industry-standard software and hardware. Students are introduced to image manipulation, and vector design visualization. No drawing skills are required. This course is designed to give an intensive overview of how graphics are created on the Apple computer using Adobe Photoshop and Illustrator. Students will be able to demonstrate an understanding and appreciation of graphic design as a form of art, demonstrate an ability to use design principles, and integrate them into projects. Students will develop creative strategies and use problem-solving techniques. In conclusion, students will finally have a diverse body of work that demonstrates both computer software knowledge and a basic sense of design.

PREREQUISITES

If you have the slightest interest in graphic design, this book is for you. In a short period of time, this foundational introductory course of creating digital art using industry-standard software and hardware will embark you on a journey that can help students understand the fundamentals in computer graphics. Gifted illustrators seeking new ways of utilizing their skills will be intrigued by the challenging design projects. Keep your cell phone close by and have fun!

DIGITALLY ENHANCED PUBLICATION

CONTENTS

ADOBE PHOTOSHOP

ADOBE ILLUSTRATOR

My greatest creations are my daughters; and an artist's work is never done.

FOREWORD

On February 10, 2022, I planned an experiential learning task to add to my Information Design capstone project. The challenge was to create workbook chapter assignments with travel literature from an Intro to Computer Graphics syllabus. My experience in Rio de Janeiro, Brazil, informed narrative stories in each chapter. The students will create design assets inspired by the data collected. Before planning, the first questions I asked myself were: What will be the purpose of going to Rio? What will I do when I get there, and how can I survive in a country without knowing the language or understanding the culture to document information. Well, the objective is to replicate my experience and reverse-engineer design assignments. That focus guided the preliminary research about the country. Copacabana's beach town was mesmerizing when I finally made it there, making it a great learning experience.

INTRODUCTION

Imagine being surrounded by volcanic rock and tropical trees in the Jurassic Era. Copacabana has the scent of Atlantic sea salt trapped in the mist every morning. When I watched the sun rise for the first time, it peeled the dead skin from my face—with innate communication, the black sea vultures came from the dark mountains, behind buildings of the mainland, and surrounding islands circling 500 meters above the beige sandy beach. Their silhouettes resemble pterodactyls. The scene there was poetically beautiful.

Daylight
In bad dreams
In a cool world
Full of cruel things
Hang tight
All you
Nothing like a big bad bridge
To go burnin' through

Being in Rio was like riding waves that led me into my first graphic design publication and a life-changing business venture—with the crushing ocean water chasing behind me, sliding my fingers to the barrel walls of the sea, capturing data, and navigating through it all to tell the story. My arrival to Brazil felt epic to begin the "Shepherd's Crook, Design Gráfico," a narrative arc workbook for students interested in the graphic design industry.

The trip to Rio de Janeiro challenged my skills in project management and capturing data for Shepherd's Crook. Food, clothing, and shelter were the bare necessities for my survival. The barrier of language, mobilization, and telecommunication is not any less essential but made for scary moments during my visit. When these things break down and your support system is over 4,000 miles away, the only thoughts in mind are not to make things worse than what they are. The distractions of recreation and government regulations were levees I had to overcome to complete the data collection process. Copacabana is the most popular beach globally, and traveling there makes it most intriguing in the middle of summer because of the inviting tourist attractions. It's fair to assume COVID-19 would have deterred the festivities and made people more cautious about life—it wasn't the case. The workbook's focus and my discipline were contested in Rio, unquestionably.

The information I collected from the trip was invaluable. Brazilians I met were both pleasant and not so pleasant but enriched with knowledge. Political conversation with English-speaking locals was unavoidable, and I was able to be very diplomatic despite my blunt personality. The interviewing plan for artists and locals was to ask open-ended questions, watch, and listen. The artist interviews and their work made it more compelling for the workbook design challenges. My tacit knowledge in observation and data collection studies opened the floodgates to qualitative data, almost too much to gather. Observations gave me immediate ideas for the city of Rio de Janeiro's infrastructure issues that could change life in Copacabana.

Rio has a personality undiscovered. I learned to take people's comments with a grain of salt if they haven't visited — even then, ten days was too short of a visit to know what's happening within a country. Rio is truly the land of creativity and a tragic place for artists. The visit will bring a unique perspective to the Shepherd's Crook. There will be difficulty in portraying what I experienced in the publication, but a referenced music score with distinct descriptions with imagery will be featured to bring the story to life. The purpose is to have the readers witness enlightenment in the computer graphics instructions.

Adobe Photoshop

CHAPTER 01
The Venture Begins

THE IDEA IN BRIEF | Adobe Photoshop

First get to know the *Mac keyboard shortcuts, menu bar* and *sub-menus, dock* and *applications, mouse-overs,* and *right-clicking.* Project expectations, review syllabus, and handouts. *Archive* and organize project folders. The importance of *citing sources* and *copyrights.* Download your lesson files for *Adobe Photoshop, Classroom in a Book.*

- **Concept Lecture:** Lay of the Land, The *design brief* and *rubric.* Pixel-based images designed for the web and its dynamics.

In elementary school, I found the globe fascinating. The entire world and its continents were captured and displayed on this interactive sphere. Spinning it and trying to pronounce the spelling of all the countries I could visit was a fantasy at age 10. There were so many interesting places. Logically it would be impossible to visit them all. Being selective would make the trips affordable and less of a challenge. I was a poor kid in one of the most impoverished places in my country. But, that wouldn't stop me from trying. How can I possibly make it to any of these places other than the neighboring states here in the United States? Now as in adulthood, I've learned a lot now that is all possible. Life has been a roller coaster of challenges as a graphic artist over the years, and I intend

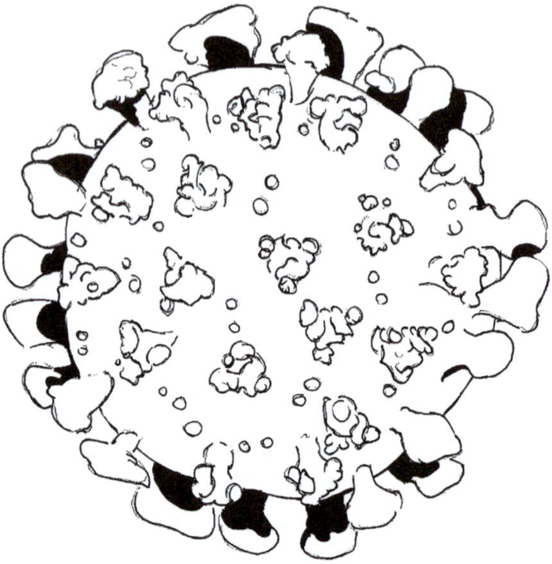

to explore more of what the world has to offer. Watching the signs to my divine path has brought me here to write this interactive workbook and teach at my local community college.

My twenty-year graphic art business came to a halt in 2020. Four days before my birthday, the president declared COVID-19 a national emergency and shut the country down. Quarantine was the only option to help slow the spread of the SARS-2 virus,

and the world began to panic over food and disinfected products. All I can do is watch my design business collapse after rebuilding it after the 2008 economic crash and car accident. After President Trump took office, I started inquiring about a contingency plan for my career and looked after new opportunities.

I inquired about a project management certificate at the local job center. It's required to take a few assessment tests to understand better placement and a job market, and the MBTI was one of them. Project management was a perfect career path, like detective work, architecture, engineering, education, graphic arts, and law. The process was quickly placed on hold.

Though it became a hopeful new beginning, quarantine was upon us, and marketing was the last thing business owners, and C-level executives were

thinking about. What was I to do? Over the years, I've set aside many personal projects, all of which I have incorporated to design in some form of art, publications, handmade furniture making, all of which I had started because of the lack of projects and all work from clients.

Browsing social media for inspiration was nothing new, so being home all day, my use of social media increased. One day scrolling on Facebook, I noticed someone selling repertory masks. Oh, I thought this was a perfect opportunity to get back into the market and design; why not? It was just a low-level surgical mask — the only thing known at this point for the pandemic. Why not jazz it up a little? Patterns can make things a little fun. Instead of plain black, blue, or white, we add some geometric patterns. So I reached out to the woman to find out that her location is Brazil. What a bummer! Encouraged, I still reached out to her. The only problem is that she only posted in Portuguese. Determined not to miss this perfect opportunity, Google translator and I began to display; How are you. I'm contacting you from the United States. Are you selling these products?" "Oh," I said in Portuguese, and the adventure began.

Social Distancing
Stand Here

LAY OF THE LAND

INTRODUCTION TO PHOTOSHOP

JOSÉ CARLOS DE BRITO E CUNHA (JULY 18, 1884 - OCTOBER 2, 1950)

Cartoonist, Illustrator, Graphic Designer

José Carlos de Brito e Cunha, known as J. Carlos, was a Brazilian cartoonist, illustrator, and graphic designer. J. Carlos also did sculpture, wrote vaudeville plays, wrote lyrics for samba, and was a significant talent in Brazilian Art Deco graphic design.

Carlos was born and died in Rio de Janeiro. His first work, a drawing of a newcomer, was published in 1902 in the magazine *Tagarela.* He collaborated in design and illustration in all the major publications of Brazil from the 1900s until the late 1940s, including O Malho, O Tico Tico, Fon-Fon!, Careta, A Cigarra, Vida Moderna, Para Todos, Eu Sei Tudo, Revista da Semana, and O Cruzeiro. His oeuvre is estimated to be more than 100,000 illustrations, with various fictionalized personages and famous Brazilian figures of the time.

FIG 1-1

ASSESSMENT

Make the design connection. Answer the nourisher's and discuss them.

1. True or False: The woman Dyshann Anderson reached out to a Brazilian Businessman. (Choose one)

- True
- False

2. Why was Dyshann's graphic art business put on hold? Choose the correct answer(s).

☐ There was an economic crash.

☐ Anderson had a personal emergency.

☐ The COVID-19 pandemic occurred.

☐ There weren't enough clients to keep the business running.

3. Brainstorming and conceptualizing what information would need to complete a design brief is the best way to start a design project. (Choose one)

- Strongly agree
- Agree
- Neutral
- Disagree
- Strongly disagree

4. Why did Anderson open up the chapter by speaking about a globe? What significance might it hold in Chapter 1 and the rest of the book? (Discuss)

FIG 1-2

THE CHALLENGE | Lay of the Land

Design Brief:

A design brief is a one-page document that provides a designer with a basic description of a design problem. A design brief usually contains a list of constraints and criteria for the problem. The design brief can also provide additional information to the designer about the needs of the client or end user.

Archiving/Submitting: Suitcase folders (L.Name-F.Name-ProjectName)

- **Image:** *(native files)*
- **Research:** *(Internet research, drawings, and stock images)*
- **Fonts:** *(alternative to system fonts used)*
- **Finished:** *(completed file for critique and deployment)*

Hot Keyboard Shortcuts: Apple, Adobe Photoshop

CHAPTER 02
The Businesswoman

THE IDEA IN BRIEF | Adobe Photoshop

Discuss *RGB vs CMYK* as they pertain to the bitmap image and pixels. Start familiarizing yourself with Adobe Photoshop — open a file, the *Menu Bar,* and menu items. Learn more about Photoshop *selection tools* and techniques, and get familiar with *Layers*, and the *Type Tool*. Explore the layers panel — *ordering, naming, moving, duplicating, locking and unlocking, sub-menus, and buttons.*

- **Concept Lecture:** Photo editing, brainstorming and conceptualization, reading and writing a design brief.

Living under quarantine was a struggle, but the quiet time alone was enjoyable. I've been trying to remove toxic people from my life for years, and it was the perfect solution. Sleep deprivation had ended, and work hadn't impeded my personal life. It was strange not hearing the vehicles on the highways in the mornings. My neighborhood is generally quiet; at times the birds weren't out moving around in a confused mass. Very surreal.

Pollution of the ocean and sky is great but the global quarantine didn't stop me from working. This was the opportunity to reorganize my life and complete my master's in information design. My sign construction project was placed on hold, but we returned back to work in a couple of weeks. Materials were scarce because national distribution channels were drying up. There was one client that kept me busy in quarantine. We designed a guidebook for the island of Saint John. Other than that, I was like everyone else in the majority of the country… taking the opportunity to be safe at home.

Before the pandemic, there were signs of something big to come. Nonprofits were struggling with funding their projects. The public sector stopped purchasing, and the private sector took a painstaking approach to its marketing dollars. Since the lease to my design studio was up for renewal, I decided to downsize and work in a shared space in downtown Hartford, Connecticut. A town once thriving with new business and tech people, it was now empty corridors and meeting rooms. Imagine 300,000 ft.^{2} of space with one guy and a laptop. I told one of my clients that there's always a party in my head the other day. God has blessed me with the ability of self-reliance.

Being reliant on one's own powers and resources rather than those of others is great, but I read somewhere that it's toxic behavior and should be used

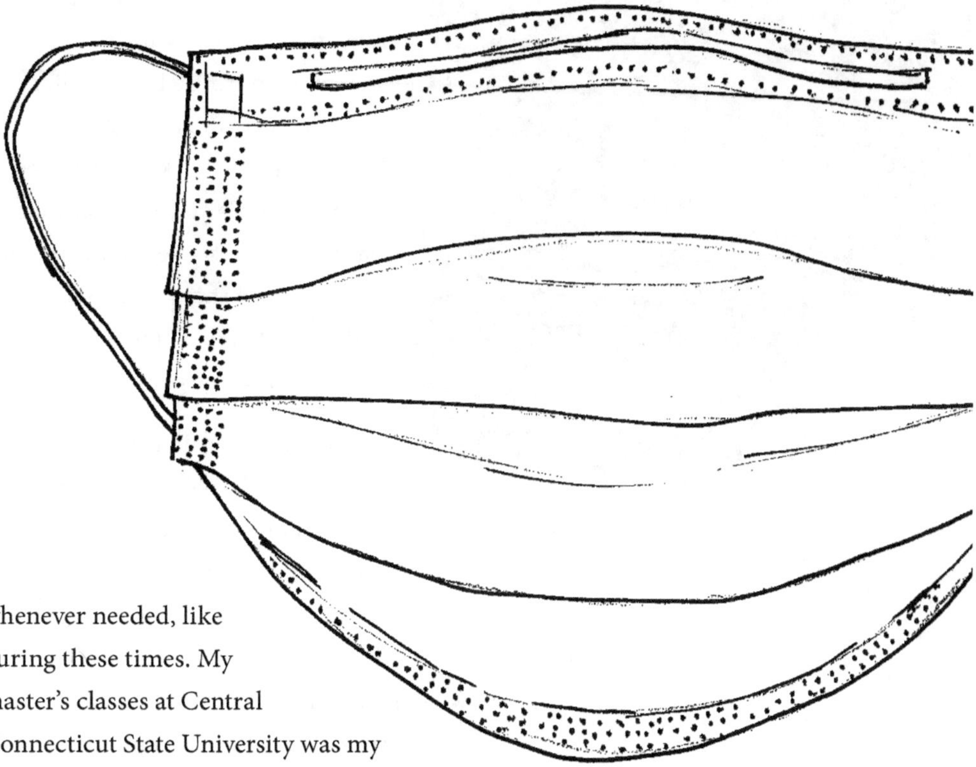

whenever needed, like during these times. My master's classes at Central Connecticut State University was my social time aside from my kids, a handful of friends, and Juliana, the Brazilian businesswoman. Spending a couple of hours chatting a day was pretty cool. We spoke about business and the current state of our countries during a pandemic. These turn into weeks and weeks turn into months. That year I really got to know Juliana. Her past experience in learning English made it easier to communicate via text and voice message. After correcting her a few times, I had the idea of teaching her for an hour on Saturdays. I didn't have set materials, but I did keep a folder of magazines and basic words on general subject matter like colors, kitchen appliances, and so forth.

The magazines were a great way to get acquainted. People's magazines were the most used because of the food sections and random pics of celebrities doing

everyday things like walking dogs or waving hello. Studying each photo references different things like, "The woman is wearing a blue sweater." Short sentences were great in the beginning. She quickly picked up common words and was excited to learn every week. We used video chat to study when she wasn't confused and frustrated speaking English. Slowly we became good friends.

She sold items on-line, but her main business work is bikinis. Juliana is a retired model and experienced fashion designer. Juliana's profile wasn't full of professional photos. She shared plenty of images and news clippings of her work with me. Juliana's worldwide network for fashion is huge, and it's what made her famous on social media platforms. Travel has been on my radar, but I really didn't have the time nor the network. Her stories inspired me to look beyond Hartford County. My research began, and I found ways to move about the world to build a global clientele. During the past 20 years, building my business and raising children have been the foundation. The idea is to leverage my skill set to work in different countries temporarily, for three months for the most part. My project management certification and teaching are the best options to expand in business.

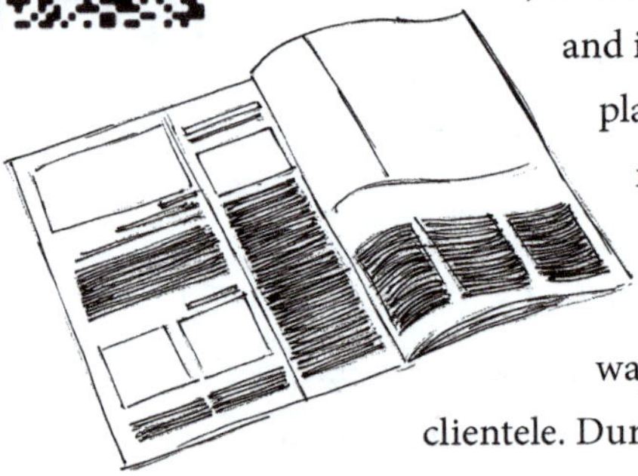

My days were full with designing future ventures and conversations with Juliana then end up riding home alone on an empty interstate highway.

PHOTO EDITING

FELIPE DANA | Photojournalist

Felipe Dana (born August 15, 1985) is a Brazilian photojournalist for the Associated Press (AP). He is known for covering social inequality, urban violence in Latin America, and conflicts in the Middle East. Dana received World Press Photo awards in 2013 and 2017 and participated in the first World Press Photo Masterclass in Latin America in 2015. He was part of the Associated Press team's finalists for the Pulitzer Prize in 2017, 2018, 2019, and 2021. In 2019, he was named Agency Photographer of the Year by The Guardian and Ibero American Photographer of the Year by POYi Latam. He has also earned numerous awards from Pictures of the Year International (POYi), the National Press Photographers Association (NPPA), the Overseas Press Club of America (OPC), and others. His drone footage of the Battle of Mosul in Iraq opens the action film Mosul on Netflix.

FIG 2-1

ASSESSMENT

Make the design connection. Answer the nourisher's and discuss them.

1. True or False: The island of Saint John is located in the Caribbean Sea and is the largest of the 3 U.S. Virgin Islands. (Choose one)

- True
- False

2. At what university did Dyshann Anderson complete a master's degree? Choose the correct answer(s).

☐ University of Hartford

☐ Eastern Connecticut State University

☐ Central Connecticut State University

☐ Yale

3. Social media platforms and Photoshop images are the best way to promote your business. (Choose one)

- Strongly agree
- Agree
- Neutral
- Disagree
- Strongly disagree

4. Anderson emphasized the importance of self-reliance. How might self-reliance benefit a graphic design business, and how can it become toxic if overused? (Discuss)

FIG 2-2

THE CHALLENGE | Photo Editing

Design Brief/ Scope:

Students must find and edit three photos with the techniques lectured in class. Use a printout to plan out the strategy. It's expected for students to use the lessons covered in the course textbook. Find tools reviewed during the lecture in the syllabus.

Specifications:

File Size: 8.5 × 10in.

Art-board: Single-sided

File Type: Ps / .Ai

Design for: Print / Web

Fished File: Save as a .pdf file.

Submitting: Suitcase folders (L.Name-F.Name-ProjectName)

CHAPTER 03
Game Plan

THE IDEA IN BRIEF | Adobe Photoshop

Learn about selecting and tools — *Magic Wand*, *Select by Color*, the *Marquis* tool — *Select by Shape*, and the *Quick Selection* tool. Edit your selection — moving, resizing, refining edges. Manipulate and *Transform* selections. Move selections from one document to another. Use the *Color Picker* on the tool panel and add color to the selections. More about *Gradient*, *Eyedropper*, and color replacement *Brush* selections. Learn image correction in Adobe Photoshop and *Camera Raw*. Explore *Adjustment Layers* for image correction and the *Healing* tools. Explore the image correction features of Camera Raw and compare.

- **Concept Lecture:** Photographing original images and how to use hidden camera phone features.

The world was crumbling before my eyes; 2020 was a frantic year. President Trump is downplaying the COVID-19 virus. The story of the death rate was reported daily, state by state. Domestic violence increases. California is battling devastating brush fires. Football stadiums were empty during the season. The MeToo Movement exposed the rich and famous. An explosion shocks Beirut and destroys the city for almost a mile. The quarantine placed great stress on people, and divorce cases increased. The news was filled with protest events because of the George Floyd murder. The level of disrespect for one another is unreal; everyone is losing their patients, and here I am again on an empty highway at 9 AM heading to work.

Day in and day out, it's just a security guard and myself in an empty seventeen-storied building.

Keeping my distance from people, using natural medicines, exercising, and eating a lot better have kept me occupied. Over the years, I've been neglecting my athletic body—telling myself it can wait another year to get back into shape after things come together for the business. In a way, I have. Replacing sugar intake was the first thing, followed by soda and rice, and then candy. The body shouldn't be working hard digesting while you sleep. During the first three months, I lost 17 pounds by eliminating sugars alone. The immune system has to work when fighting the COVID-19 virus, so I added zinc, organic ginger tea, turmeric tea, and garlic supplements to my daily dose of vitamin D, omega-3,

iron, vitamin C, and beetroot. Apple cider vinegar and ginger root tea were altered every night before bed.

Foods that would replenish lost fluids while dieting made me dehydrated. I started eating foods that were high in vitamins which my body was lacking. By March 2020, I was fully informed about my diet with an archive collection of natural remedies.

Imagine not finding enough natural things to eat for a 6'2", 250-pound football linebacker. Alfred "Dr. Sebi" Bowman, a Honduran herbalist, recommended that I understand mucous membranes buildup. So I researched the causes, eliminated dairy, and cut back on meats. An occasional steak but pork was defiantly off-limits. Baked chicken, turkey, and fish were my protein intake and shakes on workout days.

At this point, I was ready for the gym. My doctor recommended that I walk daily for 20 minutes, and I did for more than an hour. Records of blood work for deficiencies gave me a head start on supplements. I've read somewhere that eating close to bedtime wasn't a good idea. There, I solved the food and dependency problem, but here, thanks to COVID-19, the gym was off-limits.

I was determined to avoid catching the COVID-19 virus. A vaccination was months away, and I was terrified, rightfully so. Given the history of the African American males and the CDC, my skepticism was on high alert.

The idea of traveling for business would be fully sorted out before the pandemic was over, so I thought. By May, I had tons of information on several locations where I could restart my business globally.

Brazil made the most sense. At the time, there wasn't a lot of information on the country other than Wikipedia and on-line travel guides. A grassroots perspective is what I was looking for. Juliana was there but not necessarily a resource at the time, and I didn't want to inundate her personal space with questions about Rio.

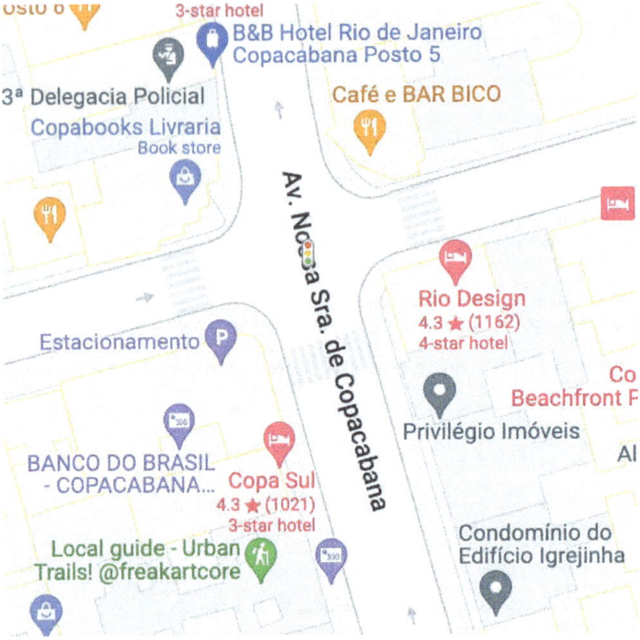

I started digging a little deeper into Brazil, the largest South American county in the western hemisphere.

As a child, the most amazing images came from carnivals. According to my local Portuguese friends, Brazilians are colorful and happy people. An annual event takes place in the coastal city-state of Rio de Janeiro. Rio has a broken world record for the largest mural in the world. The brand campaign for the 2016 Summer Olympics was amazing. My on-line research on Brazilians didn't lead to general opinions about Americans. Speaking to my professor gave some insight into what could be offensive in visiting other countries, and it is important to understand proper etiquette.

In my experience, it takes three months to know a work environment; how can I do it in a month or reduce it to days? Finding an interpreter was the best solution for the language barrier. There are American businesses in Brazil, but I was curious about what it would be like to work there. Google maps help me to explore the streets around the suitable hotels. The hotels that didn't have an American flag or referenced English-speaking front desk employees were eliminated. I kept tabs on the weather patterns and later concluded that the seasons are the opposite below the equator. If it's winter here in New England, I have to pack shorts; in Brazil it's more like spring. I have to pack suits and business casual clothing. Living comfortably in another country with little communication with locals is ideal, and based on my spending here in the

United States, I've learned it would cost me roughly $3000/ $15499.20 to live there on a monthly basis, roughly.

An emergency can happen, so I planned not to do anything physically risky. Nevertheless, I thought the worst and developed contingency plans. Robbed, stabbed, shot dead, and how my body will get back and buried were all on the list. According to Google, Brazil has the seventh-highest crime rate globally, with exceptionally high rates of violent crimes. The only way to get in and out of the country was via plane or boat. There was no train system, but only the Pan American highway on the other side of the country. Food and water was my main concern, and how would I get them without a wallet? Being stuck in a foreign country would be trippy, but how would I survive?

The information kept me compiling, and one idea led to the next. Every opportunity was pure speculation. The more I thought about the scenarios, the more I researched and the better the contingency plan ahead. I didn't stop until a reasonable solution was found for each problem. The theories created have to be tested somehow.

COMBINING IMAGES

ANANDA NAHU | Aerosol Artist, Painter, Printmaker

Ananda Nahu is a Brazilian aerosol artist born in Bahia, Brazil, in 1985. In 2001, she moved from Juazeiro to Salvador, where she attended the College of Design in 2003 and the Fine Arts School at the Federal University of Bahia in 2004. Throughout this time, she developed interests in diverse artistic expressions such as photography, and engravings as a result of her studies and research on lithography, serigraphy, and metal graving.

Nahu was introduced to aerosol art when she met artist and her husband, Rodrigo Izolag. As a result, she began using stencils to create wall art. Nahu's work primarily showcases women and utilizes various techniques, colors, visual effects, and painting styles to contribute to her vision of combining past and modern cultures and people into harmonious compositions that express pure beauty, strength, and positivity from the nature of human beings.

FIG 3-1

ASSESSMENT

Make the design connection. Answer the nourisher's and discuss them.

1. True or False: Brazil has the seventh-highest crime rate globally. (Choose one)

- True
- False

2. Based on Anderson's spending habits, what is the cost for him to live in Brazil monthly? Choose the correct answer(s).

☐ $2000 / R-$10,693.60

☐ $4000 / R-$21,387.19

☐ $3000 / R-$15499.20

☐ $5000 / R-$26,733.99

3. Having a detailed plan before you move to another country is not so important because there are people worldwide to help you when there's a problem. (Choose one)

- Strongly agree
- Agree
- Neutral
- Disagree
- Strongly disagree

4. Why is it important to focus on one's physical health while running a business and dealing with a global pandemic? Dyshann combined teas and supplements to boost his immune system; what else could he have done to protect himself? (Discuss)

FIG 3-2

THE CHALLENGE | Combining Images

Design Brief:

Combining Images Poster: Students need to design **a movie poster** by editing and combining images. Use a graph paper to research and plan out the strategy. It's expected for students to use the lessons covered in class and in the textbook. Find the tools covered in the syllabus.

Scope:

The combining images project is a poster about a superhero movie. Try to make it appear as official as possible by using large high-resolution images, good copy, and effects. Logos and credit copy is optional. Use collected copy like dates and featured actors to add details similar to an authentic movie poster. Notes from the ***Combining Images Poster*** lecture may be helpful.

Specifications:

File Size: 8.5 × 11in.
Art-board: Single-sided
File Type: Ps
Design for: Print
Finished File: Save as a .jpeg file.
Submitting: Suitcase folder (L.Name-F.Name-ProjectName)

CHAPTER 04
Simulation

THE IDEA IN BRIEF | Adobe Photoshop

Review selected techniques. Review transform tools. Review blending colors, exploring *Blend Modes* in the layers panel, and adding *Layer Styles, Warps,* and *Filters.* Learn about *Adjusting* image color and *Matching* colors using *Eyedropper* tool. Learn about gradient, paint bucket, and swatches.

- **Concept Lecture:** *Scanning* original art. How to use these tools and techniques for image correction and then creating transitioning into gray-scale and *Duotones.* The *Pantone Matching System,* design in fashion and *Color Theory* review.

Aged fingers slid away from the gurney sheets. There were rows of refrigerated trailers of COVID-19 virus victims in makeshift morgues outside New York City hospitals. This moment was captured all over broadcast stations and sent people into panic worldwide as the death toll surged.

The moment reminded me of a childhood memory of a pit bull biting down with brutal force on my foot. At seven years old, my resistance to fight back was useless; a damaged foot was inevitable and I was locked in a situation, helpless and with no way out. Similar to that sense of pending doom at the time. I had seen all the signs with this epidemic and it was finally here. I had seen all the signs, and it was finally here. While I watched the breaking news mesmerized in Walmart, a middle-aged African guy interrupted and said, "I like what he has to say." He nodded toward another TV screen, watched President Trump making a statement, and when the President was through, grinned, turned, and pushed his half-empty shopping cart to go in the opposite direction away from me. Most of us alive today have never lived through a pandemic. I felt sick to my stomach just thinking about it, and especially since I thought this was the beginning of a long nightmare. Meat and toiletries of all things had to be controlled and rationed among shoppers.

"Small minds discuss other people — gossips, good minds discuss events, and great minds discuss ideas." — Denzel Washington

Jackie and I are growing on each other. We've been talking every day, telling personal stories, and sharing compassion in design. Our work relationship on-line seems to be going well. We accomplished a lot in the past two years. We've worked on real estate websites and created the bikini site for her business just to name a few. The plan was for us to work together, with her designs, manufacturing , distribution, and marketing on my end.

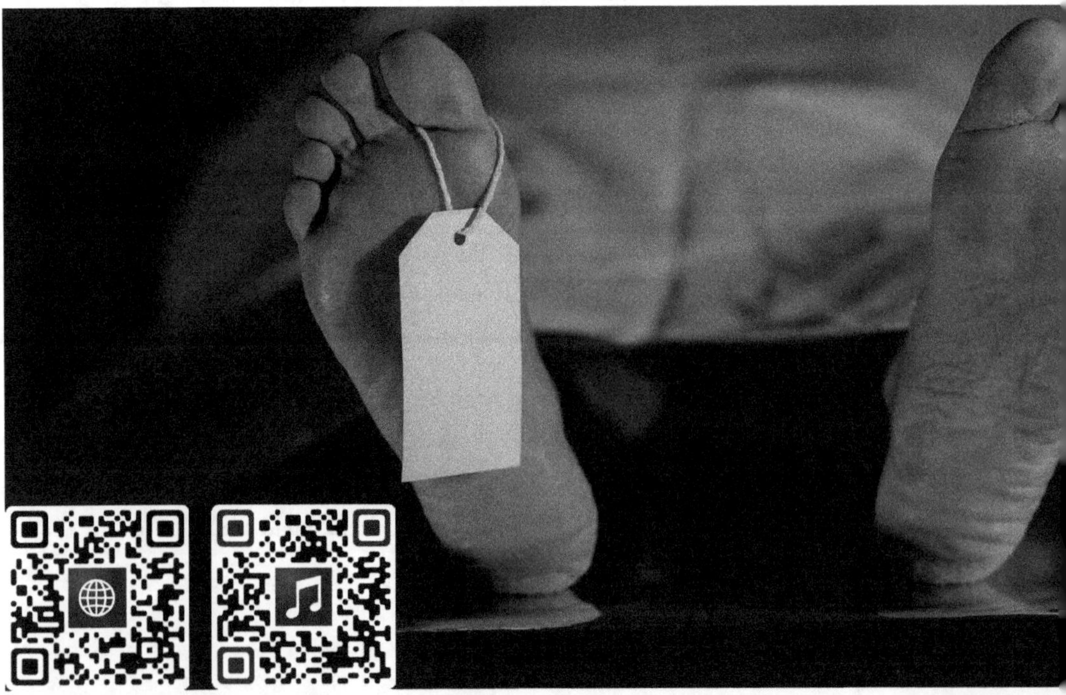

In March, she celebrated her birthday seven days after mine. Juliana stuns me with a question.

> [3/23/20, 12:12:19 AM] Juliana: Do you like my physical?
>
> [3/23/20, 12:28:16 AM] Dyshann: Yes, you have a strong physical.

Since March 2020 in-person contact has been limited because of the pandemic. We have found each other by working on projects and maintaining our businesses virtually. A platonic relationship was building. The situation worked out because my hands were full with school work, teaching, business, daughters, and life. At 40 years of age, most women will be opposed to not being in physical contact. During the pandemic, we didn't have a choice. My instincts about her and potential relationships that she might have in Rio were spot on. As a skeptic in general, I enjoy watching situations play themselves out. You can't control people and what they do; why worry about it? I'm not in harm's way, and it's just conversation. Why not let it happen? Since my separation from my kids' mother, trusting people has not been high on the priority list. I would have to be in Brazil for things to get serious, and she knew it. Social distancing is excellent at this point. With Juliana being miles away, the situation seems too perfect, so I just let it happen.

> [8/16/21, 10:14:19 AM] Juliana: Let's meet in Miami.
>
> [8/16/21, 10:16:33 AM] Dyshann: Okay. Send me the dates for four-day weekend.
>
> [8/16/21, 10:17:07 AM] Juliana: OK.
>
> [8/16/21, 10:17:10 AM] Juliana: I look.
>
> [8/16/21, 10:46:14 AM] Dyshann: Why Miami? I don't know Miami.

On September 23, 2021, Juliana randomly changed plans to let me believe she was meeting in Miami. My instincts kicked in again, and I thought she would

cancel, and she did. She called me every day I was there, so we didn't miss a beat, but I took this opportunity to test my research on working abroad. I told her not to worry, I will be in Rio for New Year. The simulation was a short 5-day trip. I've been there but never explored options and examined the city for relocation. My total experience was just vacation.

The day had arrived, and travel to Miami was great. I scheduled car repairs at Black Rock Auto Repair in Berlin, Connecticut, and walked around the building onto the train station. I gave Mike, the owner, a heads up that I would pick up the Jeep in five days on my return from Miami. He was okay with it. I timed my ride to Hartford, then to Bradley International Airport perfectly. The attendant didn't ask me for my negative COVID-19 information during the check-in. Check-in today was extremely slow, and security was tight. American Airlines charged $30 for my large bag and waived the carry-on, which may be something I should keep in mind. I wore an all-black Adidas jumpsuit with a pair of Birkenstock's and socks. It's easier to slip them off through the metal detectors. Early arrival for the flight gave me time to spare; I grabbed a smoothie from Jamba Juice and explored the thermals until boarding.

The travel transition from flight to vehicle rental and then to hotel was seamless; problems happened at Airbnb Hotel. The hotel had additional administration fees and charged $50 a day for parking. The miscommunication dealing with Airbnb and its cost was noted. It was midnight, and I was stuck in a hotel lobby trying to decide if I should pay for administration fees or find somewhere else to stay for the next five days. I was livid, so I scoured the Internet for a last-minute deal and drove down AAA Avenue and ended up at Regency Miami Airport on 42nd, a short bridge ride away from South Beach.

The weekend was full of action. Friday, I researched information about the construction counsel, found the best restaurants in the area, and did some shopping for some things I forgot. Saturday morning, I met for a class and followed my workout regimen. I had a Cuban sandwich for lunch at Latin Cafe 2000—Lejeune and spent the rest the day hiking on the coastal trails in the Brickell neighborhood. On my path, I met a neighborhood police officer who told me that Brickell Avenue was a more affluent community and always had ongoing construction on the mansions, so some areas may be inaccessible. The locals were fishing and sailing the Atlantic ocean straddling the Rickenbacker hiking trail. Later that night, needing to refuel by the physical demands of the trail, I had dinner at Uncle Tom's Southern BBQ restaurant in Coral Gables, Florida, ordering 3 of their dinner specialties, and finishing them off still with room to spare.

Cigars shops are an excellent place to hang out and find interesting people. I had an amazing conversation with the Cuban Crafters Cigar shop owner about immigration, local politics, and how Miami is split into several distinct sections. That night the hotel club hosted a dance party which I shortly attended. On Sunday, I spent packing and pegged locations on a map I picked up at a local AAA travel location and capturing data. After branding my travel check list, I walked into the next-door seafood restaurant for Sunday Night Football. Nothing was promising for business in the five days, but I learned how to connect socially with new people in a new, unfamiliar environment.

Coming back to Connecticut in September was pretty interesting in contrast to Miami. The people and the colors were a striking contrast. In Miami, people wore bright colors, and their personalities were more expressive. Most locals spoke Spanish in Miami which was surprising, but it made sense because of the nearby Islands. My Spanish is not polished, but I can get by. Driving downtown Miami was very superficial and glamorous. I mentioned this to a woman at the train stop in Hartford, Connecticut, and realized our styles and clothing preferences have more neutral tones.

GRAYSCALE TO COLOR

FABIO SASSO | Product Designer

Fabio Sasso is a product designer based in Oakland, California, currently working for Google as a senior staff designer, leading and managing design teams responsible for Android Automotive OS.

Since joining Google in 2011, Sasso has had the opportunity to work on incredible projects, from designing Google Doodles and helping startups with Google Ventures to building new products for Shopping Express Mobile as well as leading significant products and the vision for Google Search, Google Pay, and the game's efforts of Google Play.

Sasso is also the founder of Abduzeedo, an award-winning digital publication about design and a personal project that has become the source of inspiration for millions of designers and enthusiasts, and Calmaria, an application created to help people with anxiety through a straightforward breathing exercise.

FIG 4-1

ASSESSMENT

Make the design connection. Answer the nourisher's and discuss them.

1. True or False: Anderson went to Tweed New Haven Airport to catch his flight to Miami. (Choose one)

- True
- False

2. How many days did Dyshann Anderson spend in Miami? Choose the correct answer(s).

☐ 2 days

☐ 10 days

☐ 5 days

☐ 15 days

3. Visiting another country is the best way to prepare for working abroad. (Choose one)

- Strongly agree
- Agree
- Neutral
- Disagree
- Strongly disagree

4. How did visiting Miami help Dyshann test his research on working abroad—how did color influence him? (Discuss)

FIG 4-2

THE CHALLENGE | Gray-scale to Color

Design Brief:

Gray-scale to Color Book Cover: Students need to design or redesign a **book cover** for the assignment. Use graph research paper to plan out the strategy. It's expected for students to use the lessons covered in class on the pantone color system, color theory, duotones, and in the textbook. Find the topics covered in the syllabus. Duotone technique must be used in the design along with book title and author name.

Note: Duotone is a halftone reproduction of an image using the superimposition of one contrasting color halftone over another color halftone. This is most often used to bring out middle tones and highlights of an image.

Scope:

The assignment is a design or redesigned book cover about a favorite novel or design that needs your help. Use design techniques and collected copy (text) from the book you choose to explain its content. Information from the gray-scale to color book cover lecture may be helpful. Remember the page is considered a color in this project.

Specifications:

File Size: 9 × 6in.

Art-board: Single-sided

File Type: Ps

Design for: Print

Finished File: Save as a .jpeg file.

Submitting: Suitcase folder (L.Name-F.Name-ProjectName)

CHAPTER 05
Day of Reckoning

THE IDEA IN BRIEF | Adobe Photoshop

A lesson on type and text. A discussion on finding descriptive imagery in the text. A discussion on echoing text with imagery. Review file sizes and resolution. Explain multiple versions of a composite image in the same file.

- **Concept Lecture:** *Textures, Patterns,* and *Design Elements* to level up compositions. A discussion on echoing text with imagery.

There's a cell phone lying face down underneath a box of Bacardi Lemon. I'm lying face down with my upper body sagging over the bed, letting the blood rush into my head.

Meditation was the best way for creative thinking. I later found out hanging upside down on my bed helps eliminate stress, improve brain focus and balance, and other surprising benefits. The focus was on the New Year's Eve trip to Rio and how to gain helpful information on living abroad. Juliana was torn about not making it to Miami, and I have a suspicion there is more going on with her than she reveals. The truth will reveal itself when I reach Rio. The Miami trip was eye-opening because of the many mistakes made and unforeseen problems while on the trip. Rio's plan has to be faultless. Only a day back, I felt like something was missing; I had left something behind. What was

I missing? Later that day, I realized my backup cell phone was missing. Luckily, the club manager answered it when I called the number with my primary phone. The night at the hotel event is where I accidentally left it behind.

After Miami, prepping for Rio wasn't that stressful; it became more of an opportunity. Besides finding a great deal on the flight to Rio, an acquisition editor of one of the best textbook publishing companies in the United States asked me to produce a workbook for my introduction to computer graphics class. With the chance to build on my business expansion, why not use the time to create new learning materials for my students during the trip to Rio and simulate the living experience. The adventure of visiting another country will be a practical challenge to my goal of living abroad. The data collection process used to incorporate Brazilian artists in a new publishing venture will be a great feature of the book. I had it all planned perfectly.

Work and the trip have forced me to move around in public again. The passport company gave me a malaria shot, bug repellent, and more information I overlooked. Finding the right clothes for the meetings and the weather was entirely essential. I cashed in favor with a friend who is a tailoring to get a new New Year's Eve shirt. He agreed and took my measurements. My plan was to come back to get the shirt before my flight. The translator I found decided to

help with the interviews and was open to being my guide in Rio. A block away from the beach was the Rio Design Hotel and many resources listed in the contingency plan. On the 22nd of December, the last visit I had to make was to my tailor for the shirt. The following morning, I woke up with COVID-19!

The disappointing news was delivered to Juliana. It was tough telling her I wasn't showing up for New Year's Eve. We hadn't spoken in a few days after giving her the information, and she made it apparent that she was looking forward to meeting in person for the first time. The flight, hotel, everything about the Rio trip was postponed for the 10th of February. I was home, sick, and watched the Times Square ball drop in Times Square live on my phone. After the New Year came in, I fell asleep.

The day had arrived and I started as planned, with a few exceptions. That early morning at the design studio, I printed copies of the itinerary and essential documents and kept digital reserves on my cell phone. Breakfast was just fruit. Packing on a full stomach before the fight, knowing it would be nine hours was the wrong move. Packing for the trip a week ago was a good move, so I was confident everything was sealed and ready to go. While attentively checking my list, the meter expired for two minutes and found my car ticketed for $45 for a parking violation—outstanding, racking up bills before I left the United States.

When I arrived at the commuter lot, three cars were parked in the distance from each other—a good indication that the train ride to New York will be quiet. The announcement over the loudspeakers at the station referenced a slight delay for the train. I hustled, hauling my luggage to the first elevator to the catwalk. The train was quickly approaching, and I sprinted while balancing a laptop, a carry-on in one arm, and a giant silver suitcase in the other. Being on this train would put me ahead of schedule for the 9:00-pm flight. Now dragging the luggage along, the train arrives and whistles. I anxiously waited for the platform elevator to get to the catwalk level. The door opened, and I pushed the bags in, then pressed the close-door button hysterically. Of course, the elevator took its time, then opened on the platform level, and the train slowly departed.

Thinking the next train should be arriving soon, I wasn't worried about missing the fight. It would be 12:30, and New York was only a two-hour train ride. I was wrong—the next train was at 3:30. It's a bit close, but I should arrive at the airport by 7. And I can't drive there to save time because of the unpredictable traffic. My return flight arrival is at Bradley International Airport, so traveling back to New York to retrieve the Jeep would be a hassle.

The train ride was nerve-wracking, but I arrived at around 5:30 pm, ready to hop on a shuttle to JFK. I asked Tylor, the customer services person, "Where do I catch the shuttle to JFK?" - And she said, "Hey sweetie, the shuttles were canceled because of COVID. Your best gamble is the subway. Here are the directions." Then she hands me a small third-generation copy sheet of paper with the directions and ink-written annotations. I looked at her in disappointment and thought I couldn't believe this was happening. Traffic was too busy, and the bridge had construction, which would be a bad move. Subway train was an option in my research, so I felt hopeful. Tylor said, "head in that direction," pointing to a large passageway. "You're looking for the AirTrain, and it would take you straight there."—"Straight there," I said and laughed. I knew there was no straight there in the New York subway system. I walked in the direction and saw a dark, winding staircase behind the terminal. Long story short, I lugged the up-and-down staircases and got lost twice before arriving at the AirTrain. It would be nice if bright directions and lettering were on the way there from Grand Central.

JFK International Airport was beautiful and not as crowded as I had imagined, but the situation got ugly quickly. After a couple of train rides and escalators, I found the gateway to American Airlines and saw a short, nicely dressed, brown-complexioned woman, standing at the entryway. She had just ended a conversation in Portuguese with a couple and looked in my direction, anticipating my question. "Hello," she said. "Hi, I have a flight at 9:00 pm and I'm looking to check in. I also have luggage. Is this line for Brazil?" I asked politely. "Do you have all the proper documents, Sir?" She answered. "Oh, yes, sure, here it is," I said. The Airline attendant searched the papers and said, "You are missing the ANVISA Traveler's Health Declaration confirmation form, she said, rolling her eyes. Please step aside and fill out the form on the website, then show me the confirmation email before you check in, please."

I pulled out my laptop, signed in to the local Wi-Fi, checked my email for the link, found the ANVISA email, and filled out the five-to-seven-page form. It didn't confirm the first time but on second, so I approached her again. She asked a couple about the Traveler's Health Declaration form. The guy shrugged his shoulders, and they both walked in my direction. "Are you guys having trouble with the Declaration form, too?" I said curiously. They said no, but the woman had forgotten her passport and kept walk away. A Hasidic Jewish man was standing right behind me with a young boy when I asked the couple the question. The gentleman raised his eyebrows, and I asked him, "Are you having trouble too?" The man said, "I don't speak English" in a typical New York accent. I said, "Are you serious?"—And smiled at him. The little boy smiled back but the man pulled him away going toward a long table where other passengers were filling out various forms.

At this point, it was 8:15 pm. "Calm down, the worst would never happen," I said aloud to no-one in particular. The Brazilian Declaration website finally worked. Check in was at 8:35 PM, I sprinted to the gate, grateful that experience was behind me. I found my seat, placed some items in the overhead bin, put in earplugs, and quickly fell asleep. The late-night flight to Rio went smoothly.

POETRY MONOGRAPHS

CARLOS EDUARDO FERNANDES LÉO | Street Artist

Carlos Eduardo Fernandes Léo (born January 1, 1976, in São Paulo, Brazil), known as Eduardo Kobra, nicknamed Kobra, is a street artist who officially began his career in 1987 at age 11 in his hometown of São Paulo. Since then, he has painted over 3,000 murals on five different continents. Most of the murals are commissioned, and some are original. Kobra now works with a team of artists who paint between two and four murals each month. To this day, Kobra continues to live and work in his hometown of São Paulo.

Eduardo Kobra grew up in São Paulo, Brazil's largest city. His father was a weaver, and his mother was a housewife. He attended public school at Escola Municipal Mauricio Simão. He received no official academic training but became a well-known, self-taught artist. Before starting his official art career, he enjoyed illegally tagging walls, eventually leading to several arrests throughout his teenage years.

FIG 5-1

ASSESSMENT

Make the design connection. Answer the nourisher's and discuss them.

1. True or False: Anderson went to Rio on January 3. (Choose one)

- True
- False

2. Why couldn't Anderson go to Rio in December? Choose the correct answer(s).

☐ The flight was canceled.

☐ There was a large snowstorm.

☐ The airport was shut down.

☐ He woke up with COVID-19 symptoms.

3. Multiple backup plans are overkill for a trip. Getting lost in a labyrinth subway system is a great way to utilize way-finding signage to reach the destination. (Choose one)

- Strongly agree
- Agree
- Neutral
- Disagree
- Strongly disagree

4. Despite preparing for the Rio trip, many problems appeared for Dyshann on the way to the airport. How can one have a sturdy backup plan for emergencies? Describe what adaptations made it successful in catching the flight to Rio de Janeiro. (Discuss)

FIG 5-2

THE CHALLENGE | Poetry Monographs

Design Brief:

Students need to design with a **Monograph/Poem (50-75 words max)** for a **Poster**. Use graph paper to research and plan out the strategy. Use imagery to depict the monograph/poem to show how it's relatable. It's expected for students to use the lessons on textures/patterns covered in class and in the textbook. Find the tools covered in the syllabus.

Scope:

The monograph project is a poster about a favorite poem created with a pantone color(s). Use the duotone process. Combine and edit photos so they work in your favor. Use visual inspiration to support the poem.

Specifications:

File Size: 17 × 11in.

Art-board: Single-sided

File Type: Ps

Design for: Print

Finished File: Save as a .pdf file.

Submitting: Suitcase folder (L.Name-F.Name-ProjectName)

CHAPTER 06
The Arrival

THE IDEA IN BRIEF | Adobe Photoshop

Review Photoshop features but move into a more creative space. All the tools you've learned at this point will make you better equipped to manage upcoming projects in Adobe Photoshop. Using the methodologies taught in the lectures opens up creativity. Testing your research and brainstorming skills will become problematic. Think beyond your comfort level and take chances on project ideas. Develop the Crook!

- **Concept Lecture:** Composition, *Focal Element, Structure,* and *Balance* in composition. Researching and archiving Internet images and inspiration.

There's a chocolate-stained $100 bill in a backpack. The cyclist rode up to the drive-in ATM and deposited it into his account. The bill accompanied the change he received from the Baskin Robbins cashier earlier that day. It was a triple chocolate fudge brownie that caused the mess.

At 6 AM, the stewardess woke me up with a question: "Would you like something to eat?" The sun peeks through the clouds, and my boots are completely off. I was comfortable in the emergency-exit aisle. I kicked my winter boots underneath the seats, and my pillows were tucked tightly between the seats. I had the whole row to myself. Nine hours and the economy seats would have been brutal with my old football injuries.

The landing was perfect, but the actual test would be going to the hotel from the airport. The labyrinth terminals were oddly empty, and it was a 5-to-7-minute walk to customs. The small crowd of people from the New York City flight led the way. Another five-minute walk led to luggage claim and onward to foreign currency. I managed to exchange Brazilian reals from my bank back home, but I withdrew extra money in case of an emergency. Paying the hotel in cash was necessary instead of using my traveler's card.

During my first travel planning to Brazil, I tried to pay for the hotel on-line, and it was a hassle filling out approval forms and other legal documents. The United States had to sanction Brazil because of frequent fraudulent activities on United States citizens' credit cards. The Rio Design Hotel was kind enough to let me play upon arrival.

The foreign currency teller at the airport spoke to me in Portuguese. I replied in English, "My Portuguese is poor. Do you speak English?" She gave a bizarre expression, not surprised but more baffled. She spoke in broken English,

"Would you like the small, mix, or large bills, Sir?" I responded, "Large bills, please." I handed her the cash, and she began to count. Midway through, she pulled out a $100 bill and placed it on the counter. After finishing, she said, "I can't take this bill, it's dirty." I looked at her with curiosity. Many thoughts came to mind, but I dismissed them and continued. The journey is over, and one last door passes through before the taxi stand. When I exited, I found the corridor being a massive space, as I had imagined—a crowd of people was cheering for arrivals behind a barrier. The embarrassment of wearing my winter clothes was a funny moment I will never forget. It was like 80 degrees in Rio; wearing winter boots and pushing heavy luggage wasn't ideal.

Almost instantly, taxi drivers surrounded the passengers. Finally, someone spoke to me in English. I turned to the voice of a short, brown-complexioned gentleman wearing glasses, a green uniform shirt, and khaki pants. A supervisor is looking to help me get to my destination. As planned, I handed him the address to the Rio Design Hotel, and after 30 seconds of explaining the cost, another guy sprayed my boots and began to wipe them. The man said, "Please, Sir, I need to feed my family and the favelas." I quickly gave him money and said, "Nao, gracia." "Obrigado, mi amigo," he replied. As I followed the supervisor, a woman I recalled seeing on the plane from New York gave me a kind nod and smiled.

During the ride to the hotel, I anticipated a walk around in the streets to absorb the culture. Along the way, the taxi driver and I passed by the favelas and into a vast tunnel. Copacabana is a bustling city, but it's rainy season. Some people were wearing respiratory masks, but apparently, COVID-19 never impacted the town. We passed many restaurants and small businesses at the end of the ride. Blocks away from the hotel, I saw a interesting restaurant with an open patio I wanted to visit. The Eclipse Bar Restaurante Pizzaria has open seating and appears like a sports bar.

The hotel room was perfectly furnished with an artistic chic style and very clean. I briskly unpacked, showered, and changed my clothes. Water to consume

and brush my teeth was on top of the list. The hotel workers were amicable, so I hung out and laughed it up with them for a little while before my walk at 2 PM. The valet said I could find large water bottles at the bodega around the corner.

I walked in and out of one hotel after the next. The assessment of the list of hotels that I may visit in the future was completed. The Fairmont Hotel is my favorite. Before entering the Fairmont, the lobby valet asked for COVID vaccination documentation which I presented digitally on my iPhone. The lounge was huge, and it was decorated with thick rugs and chandeliers in the dining area with a 100-foot pool. A few guys were relaxing on the deck, smoking cigars in lawn chairs with a glass of Makers Mark. At 4:30 or 5 o'clock, I arrived at the Eclipse Bar Restaurante Pizzaria and texted everyone about my safe arrival. Juliana was working and wanted to meet for dinner that night.

[2/11/22, 2:29:09 PM] Juliana: Estou em reunião

[2/11/22, 2:29:29 PM] Juliana: Vamos jantar melhor Em 40 minutos chego

[2/11/22, 2:29:31 PM] Juliana: :)

[2/11/22, 2:41:03 PM] Dyshann: Eu vou caminhar.

[2/11/22, 2:42:40 PM] Juliana: Está chovendo

[2/11/22, 2:42:56 PM] Juliana: Por isso Que não consigo chegar agora

[2/11/22, 2:43:00 PM] Juliana: Chove

[2/11/22, 2:45:50 PM] Dyshann: image omitted

[2/11/22, 2:46:10 PM] Juliana: Ok

[2/11/22, 2:46:29 PM] Juliana: Estou esperando a chuva passa

[2/11/22, 2:46:42 PM] Juliana: Para ir

[2/11/22, 2:47:28 PM] Juliana: Terminei a reunião e tive que sentar para esperar um pouco

[2/11/22, 2:47:35 PM] Juliana: Para passar a chuva

[2/11/22, 3:09:58 PM] Juliana: Esta por onde

Shortly after speaking to my family and contacts from Rio, I gave Juliana the address to the Eclipse Bar Restaurante Pizzaria, and we hung out until 8 PM.

ART OF CROPPING

CAKO MARTIN | Designer

Cako Martin is a Brazilian/Spanish designer who graduated as an industrial designer based in São Paulo. He works in graphic design, creating packaging, print, branding, web design, illustration, social media, and fine art. He also creates product lines and limited editions under partnership agreements. Cako developed special projects for companies such as Havaianas, Nestlé, Epson, Electrolux, Dove Men, Canson, Fnac, Unimed do Brasil, Nickelodeon, Vivo, Cacau Show, and TAM. In 2015, Cako launched Cako Martin Pop Shop Store, selling original art, prints, and limited editions. Cako Martin serves on an examining board team in Faculdade de Belas Artes de São Paulo for graphic, product, and interior design disciplines.

FIG 6-1

ASSESSMENT

Make the design connection. Answer the nourisher's and discuss them.

1. True or False: Anderson met with Juliana finally in person at the Eclipse Bar Restaurante Pizzaria in Brazil. (Choose one)

- True
- False

2. What did the lobby valet ask for at the Fairmont Hotel? Choose the correct answer(s).

☐ Reservation information

☐ COVID-19 vaccination documentation

☐ Driver license

☐ Payment

3. It would be best if you exchanged your currency for the country you plan to travel to before going on the trip. (Choose one)

- Strongly agree
- Agree
- Neutral
- Disagree
- Strongly disagree

4. How does Anderson settle during his first day in Brazil? What were his picture-perfect preconceptions before arriving at Brazil? (Discuss)

FIG 6-2

THE CHALLENGE | Art of Cropping

Design Brief:

Students will search and find ten images and do cropping exercises to understand design layouts better. Graph paper will be optional to plan out strategies. Students are expected to use notes on the understanding composition video viewed in class and the lessons in the textbook. Research the tools covered in the syllabus.

Scope:

Find images with Focus, Balance, and Structure.

Specifications:

File Size: 300 dpi

Art-board: 4 × 6in.

File Type: Ps

Design for: Web

Submitting: Suitcase folder (L.Name-F.Name-ProjectName)

Understanding Composition

13 Smartphone Photography tips & tricks

CHAPTER 07
Cigar Hunt

THE IDEA IN BRIEF | Adobe Photoshop

You have the web at your disposal. Being a content creator is difficult because accountability and credibility are your survival. Once you have launched information on the Internet, it's there forever. Why not create something meaningful? Develop the Crook!

- **Concept Lecture:** Storytelling and the elements to a story: the *Arc, Change, Theme, Coherence,* and *Plausibility* built into the formula in creating stories. Using panels to draw the audience deeper into the story and keeping them hooked to the end. Media ethics.

It's Saturday, February 12th. The last couple of days were a mess. Relaxing was on my mind before preparing for the week tomorrow. A cigar would be nice. There was a cigar shop on my research list not too far from the hotel. I didn't care enough to investigate the shop quality, or if they hosted a lounge. I just needed a cigar. Google recommended a ten-minute walk, so I clicked the Start button and began to walk.

The exchange began with me finding out that my Google Maps app had misled me off course again—not so disappointed this time around. Maps led me to

Shopping Cassino Atlântico, a small mall at the end of the street. Curious about what I would find there, I pushed through the single glass door and entered. This mall was step up from what I have seen so far in the neighborhood and was filled with vendors like Starbucks coffee shops, jewelry stores, and handmade furnishings. This scene is a playground for the well-to-do. The first person I encountered was a security guard, a short gentleman that I guessed to be in his sixties. He was wearing and oversized navy blue sports coat. In a calm tone, he spoke in Portuguese, "Can I help you find your way?" I said, "Sim" (yes), then I asked about cigars (tobaccia). He shrugged his shoulders, and I said, "Obrigado," (thank you) and continued to admire the handmade artwork. The mall was astonishing, so I continued to browse more deeply in the hallways. There were beautiful contemporary works of art displayed in windows around, floor after floor.

An open gallery without a curator, Gallery Patricia Costa's, sat on the top floor. Patricia's name was drawn to me because my middle name is Patrick. It was odd to find the door completely open, so I advanced consciously and then

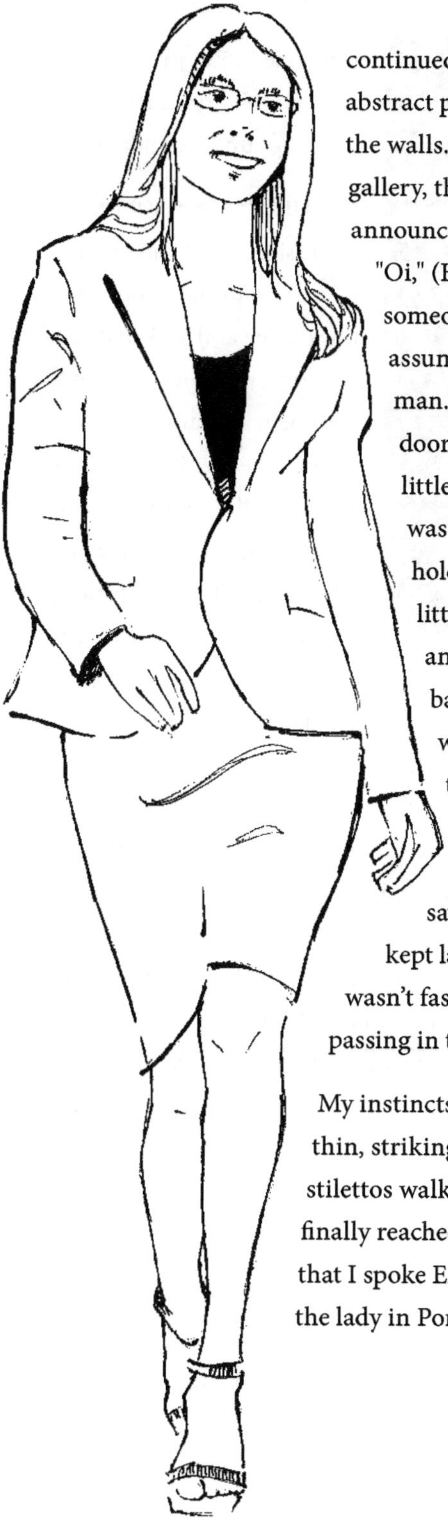

continued forward. There were portraits and abstract paintings installed randomly across the walls. Past a small desk in the back of the gallery, there was a slightly open rear door. I announced myself clearly with a stern voice, "Oi," (Hello), "is anyone there?" I heard someone rustling in behind the door. I assumed that my voice startled the young man. He quickly made his way to the door and spoke fast, in Portuguese, a little too fast for me to make out what he was saying. He appeared in his twenties, holding a cell phone in his hand. A little taken back by his exuberance and exciting body language, I mosey backward toward the entrance while he was talking to me. Shockingly enough, the security guard was waiting for us in the hallway. The two gentlemen were trying to sort out what I was saying, and the translator in my cell kept lagging. Typing on my cell phone wasn't fast enough to defuse the chatter. People passing in the hallway notice the commotion.

My instincts told me to look up to the right. A thin, striking Brazilian woman with glasses and stilettos walked toward the gallery. When she finally reached us, the security guard explained that I spoke English. The young man commented to the lady in Portuguese. The day finally arrived when

someone in Rio misunderstood me. I didn't expect it to be so soon, but understandable.

She said, "I'm sorry for the confusion. Hello, my name is Danila," and she stepped two feet toward me and looked directly into my eyes. Posturing and confident as many educated women are, her inviting words dissolved the confusion right away. I introduced myself as a fellow artist and educator here on a visiting trip to throw light on Rio's artist works for a publication. I explained it'd been a long journey. Rio de Janeiro has been on my bucket list as a child. Still, I am here to complete fieldwork for my master's in information design and simultaneously write a workbook of my experience. She was very impressed and stated she had artists that would interest me. We walked back into the gallery, and she invited me to sit. The first artist she spoke about was Leo Natsume. The artist struggled to live in a favela and now has a productive profession as a designer. Leo has launched a project that is quickly becoming popular in the art community, and it has been a benefit in his life. Artist Felipe was another artist Danila mentioned. Alex (@felipecaralho.art) is a line-art designer from her list of acquaintances who no longer live in Rio; I later found this out in a short conversation on social media. Philippe was mentioned in the conversation, but he had family obligations and could only meet via Zoom.

Over time, our conversation evolved, and we spoke for over an hour about theory, the country's current state, and how it was touched by external factors like COVID-19, then debated on the science. She mentioned Walter

Benjamin, which was one thing that caught my attention. He's a German Jewish philosopher, cultural critic, and essayist. My professor spoke of him several times in his lectures. In my observations, I noticed prominent Jewish influences like synagogues in my couple of days here and connected.

After my long walk, I hung out with Juliana by the pool, went to Carretão Ipanema Classic Grill for dinner, and discussed the next phase on the bikini business website.

STORYTELLING

LEO NATSUME | Visual Designer

Leonardo Azevedo (aka Leo Natsume) is a talented visual designer focused on Digital Design—UI/UX, interaction design, and mainly illustration, currently working at Grupo RBS, based in Porto Alegre/Brazil. He has won several prizes and gained international recognition. Leo is a freelancer and has worked for and collaborated on projects with companies like Google, Uber, Twitter, Nike, Disney, Coca-Cola, and The New York Times.

FIG 7-1

ASSESSMENT

Make the design connection. Answer the nourisher's and discuss them.

1. True or False: Anderson's visit to Gallery Patricia Costa was a bad idea. (Choose one)

- True
- False

2. What master's degree was Anderson looking to complete? Choose the correct answer(s).

☐ Graphic design.

☐ Marketing.

☐ Information design.

☐ Business.

3. Learning about artists' and designers' backstories in other countries can help inspire one's works. (Choose one)

- Strongly agree
- Agree
- Neutral
- Disagree
- Strongly disagree

4. Google Maps misled Anderson— what methods would you have taken to get back on the right path? (Discuss)

FIG 7-2

THE CHALLENGE | Storytelling

Design Brief:

Students will design a **multi-post** for **social media**. Use graph paper to plan out the strategy. It's expected for students to use the lessons covered in class and in the textbook. Find the topics covered in the syllabus.

The passion project is an Instagram Carousel multi-post about a personal story. The story can illustrate a place you've visited, a funny situation, or a joke. Use design techniques and collected or original copy to tell the story. Use graph paper to research and plan out the strategy.

Specifications:

File Size: 1080 × 1080 px

Art-board: 10 panels

File Type: .Ps

Design for: Web

Fished File: Save as a .jpeg or .png file.

Submitting: Suitcase folder (L.Name-F.Name-ProjectName)

11 Types of Instagram Content

CHAPTER 08
Lonely Knight

THE IDEA IN BRIEF | Adobe Photoshop

Adobe Photoshop video editing. *Timeline* mode, set *key-frames* in the *Timeline* panel, modify the *position*, *opacity*, or *style* such as applying *adjustment layers* and *filters* to video (even Camera RAW). Stacking *layers*, including graphics, text, and photos.

- **Concept Lecture:** Stop-motion and smear frames.

I woke up this morning in my hotel room with many responsibilities. As a person granted an honorary title of an author by one of the largest publishing companies in the United States for the service to the design industry, I had a job to complete for them and myself. Preparing for the week ahead isn't going to be easy, but I'm confident that the leads noted by Danila were incredible.

In general, my days will be structured around meetings and transcribing the outlines for the workbook. I intend to exercise every morning at 5 AM, be done at 6, shower, and be ready to start my day by 7, then study my project management course for two hours before breakfast. Rio is one hour ahead of Hartford, Connecticut, so the plan should run smoothly. I can have coffee meetings and a hotel cafeteria as planned and have lunch meetings with the artist or visit an organization or company to get a sense of the work environment. Around 3 or 4 o'clock, I will transcribe my findings, edit, and archive them for later use. When I get back to the States, I will organize the lessons according to the artist and complete the book. Dinner will be light from here on out, so I can stick to my sleep regiment at 8 PM. I plan to visit tourist sites on the weekend and be ready to go home Monday the 21st.

Before my on-line research begins, I have to set up my VPN Express account. Express VPN set up, phone service changes, and the added features were at a higher cost. The art colleges in the area were my main targets because of their prominence in Rio. As an educator, I am sure I can obtain a brief history lesson on who's doing what and where Rio intends to go in the future? Messa, my interpreter, is someone I need to rely on heavily. The strategy is to have him at every meeting and visitation as possible. I received confirmation before traveling, so every coffee meeting should go steadily. The distance between the

hotel and the organizations wasn't too far, and they were no more than 15 to 20 minutes apart.

On the other hand, the artist was miles away or no longer in the country because of opportunities. Their artwork and on-line presence are very accessible, and their phone numbers and social media handles have been collected and archived. Monday is the day to confirm or set up interviews with the artist. Messa lives 5-minutes walk from the Rio Design Hotel. If there are any problems, the translator app will help transcribe the interview.

Finishing the last of the packed food from home hinted at getting more acquainted with the neighborhood's local supermarket and sandwich shops as planned. Around 3 o'clock, a visit to the hotel lobby desk to question the manager and the workers about

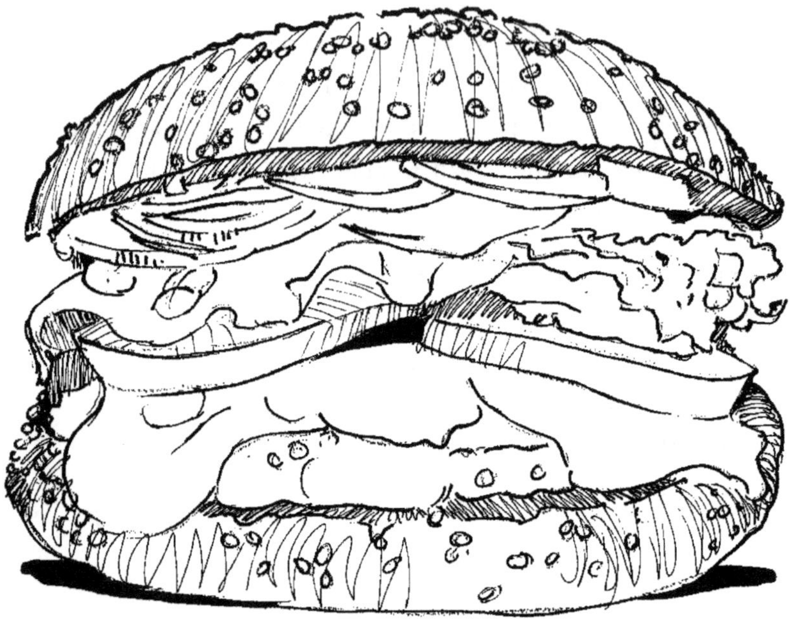

food was very helpful. They confirm the majority of the restaurants' list has excellent service. They enlightened me about the Rio Design Hotel, previously named Candido Design Hotel after a Brazilian painter. According to Wikipedia, Candido Portinari, the painter, is regarded as one of the most prominent and influential practitioners of the linear neo-realism style. I also found out that the supermarket was a block away and made sandwiches, hot pizza, and baked goods fresh daily. I walked back through the hotel lobby from the supermarket with two large shopping bags in my hand. The manager mentioned TT Burgers restaurant. The restaurant was a couple of blocks away, and I didn't mind the walk. The streets of Copacabana weren't as busy as usual, but the beach town was very scenic without cars bustling around.

After ordering my food, I realized I was eating alone. It's been done in the past, but this time it was different. My daughters hadn't called, and my friends were at home usually on Sundays watching sports. I was stuck in a foreign country trying to understand what was happening during his 'futebol' game. It's going to be a long night.

SOCIAL MEDIA GIFS

(STOP-MOTION)

FELIPE CAVALCANTE | Designer, Educator

Felipe Cavalcante graduated in design from the University of Brasília (UnB). He's one of the co-founders of Mopa, a graphic design and illustration studio. Teacher of UnB's graphic design department from 2011 to 2013, he was ahead of the disciplines of typography, illustration, and printing materials and processes. He takes part in Irmãos Colagem, a collaborative project with Júlio Lapagesse and Pedro Ivo Verçosa, developing giant collage murals. Also, Verçosa has created a screen-printed magazine *Sem/Registro*. It's one of the members of Espaço Laje, a collective studio of seven artist friends that holds productions in cinema, animation, music, drawing, painting, printing, comics, and collage.

FIG 8-1

ASSESSMENT

Make the design connection. Answer the nourisher's and discuss them.

1. True or False: Rio is one hour behind Connecticut. (Choose one)

- True
- False

2. The Rio Design Hotel was previously named Candido Design Hotel, which was referencing _______. Choose the correct answer(s).

☐ A flower

☐ A Brazilian painter

☐ A Brazilian musician

☐ A book

3. Watching footage and reading news articles is essential before visiting another country. (Choose one)

- Strongly agree
- Agree
- Neutral
- Disagree
- Strongly disagree

4. How does an illustrated schedule help Dyshann Anderson translate to action while visiting Copacabana? (Discuss)

FIG 8-2

THE CHALLENGE | Social Media .Gifs

Design Brief:

Students need to design a **.gif animation** for **social media**—a class exercise on how to use specific Photoshop features. It's expected for students to take notes and go through step-by-step exercises covered in class and in the textbook. Find the tools covered in the syllabus.

Scope:

The project is an animation about a favorite video from the Internet. Use design techniques and collected and/or written copy to depict a funny situation or joke. Information from the ***class exercise and Textbook pp. 362*** may be helpful. Use graph paper to research and plan out the strategy.

Specifications:

File Size: 500 × 500px

Art-board: Single-sided, 5 frames or more

File Type: .Ps

Design for: Web

Fished File: Save as a .gif file.

Submitting: Suitcase folder (L.Name-F.Name-ProjectName)

Flip book Exercise:

Adobe Illustrator

CHAPTER 09
Troubling Start

THE IDEA IN BRIEF | Adobe Illustrator

Lay of the Land—Introduction to Illustrator: Understanding *objects* vs. *images.* Get familiar with the *workspace, tools, menus bars, panels, art-boards*, various *document setups*, and *file formats*. Explore the use of *rulers, grids, set templates* option, and *guides.*

- **Concept Lecture:** Working with *vector-based* images designed for print media.

A small hand and arm stretch into a tight sewer guard, reaching for a cross pendant in the black of night lit by an old fluttering street lamp. Fingernails scratched the surface of the steel walls, and a voice hopelessly grunted with no one there to help.

Going to bed early last night allowed me to see the sunrise for the first time; the morning had many surprises. I was sitting up on the bed anxiously to work out. My teeth felt strange. I use my tongue to feel around my teeth's inner and outer surface, rubbing left to right. I ran into the bathroom and stared into the mirror, terrified at my teeth. I didn't notice anything unusual, but the enamel feels like it's been deteriorating. The bottled water read "Mineral Water." Unaware of the harsh chemicals used to purify this water, I used it to brush my teeth. My dentist has suggested using a soft brush because of the amount of force used when brushing. The combination wasn't beneficial. Before taking a walk to the beach, I'll purchase a bottle of water used in most restaurants. It had a blue label.

After refreshing up, I headed to the beach to watch the sunrise. It was only a block's walk away from the hotel. While walking, the stench of human feces assaulted my nose halfway down the block, something I hadn't seen before, and spotted a homeless couple sleeping cuddled on a piece of cardboard. The woman wore red and white shorts, and the highly skinny man was without a shirt and wearing jean shorts. The couple was without shoes and young, roughly around their mid-20s. One thing that was unforgettable about the young man was his toenails. They were at least an inch long, muddy, thick, and worn. It wasn't the first time to see homeless people, but my Rio friends and interpreters warned me. Witnessing it for the first time was humbling and made me more grateful.

Not completely dark out, the sun was peeking out from beyond the open Atlantic ocean. Very few people were moving about the streets, and people were scattered throughout the beach. A man was pulling a 6 × 9 cart full of beach chairs. The business owner struggled to the street corner and began unloading the cart. Crossing the long, once-busy intersection, I found a place to sit along the cobblestone fence just before the beach area. On the way there, I did notice an underground staircase with signage labeled "banheiro" with symbols relating to man and woman posted on the wall of the staircase. I wondered why portable restrooms on a beach this huge weren't noticeable.

Watching the sunrise in Rio is fantastic. Collecting my thoughts and daydreaming, I stared at the waves crashing into the beach. While thinking about people and what I had planned for the week, I was interrupted by slow sandy footsteps and unfamiliar energy. It startled me a little. I glimpsed and saw someone standing and staring at me from behind. She took a step forward, and I shuffled around to face her. It was a teenager; she must have come out from the staircase below. People don't naturally approach me because of my appearance and quiet demeanor. For her to stand this close to me was unusual. The shabby appearance of her clothes stated that she had been homeless for a while. The light-brown-complexioned girl had sticky leftover

food around her mouth and round cheeks. Her tangled hair had small sticks and leaves trapped between her curls. For a moment, waiting and staring at each other, I cautiously knew that she wanted something from me. I was staring intensely into her eyes, searching for her intentions.

People have told me several times that I unconsciously stare at people. My ex used to say, "It feels like you're walking around in my soul when you stare at me like that. It's almost like you know what I'm thinking." Well, this is one of those moments, and the energy I felt from the teenager was unstable, undeveloped, and slowly becoming recognizable. Yes, similar to my daughter at age two. Then, she finally said something, but I couldn't understand what she said in Portuguese. She lifted her arms slowly to gesture to the water bottle on the wall next to me, then folded her hands in prayer. Rolled up in her left hand, she held a broken necklace. My chest felt tight, and my heart heavy, filled with blood. I remained speechless. As fast as possible, I stood up, handed her the water, and quickly walked away—Being there another moment would have brought me to tears.

It was 14th of February, Valentine's Day, and Jacqui and I agreed to work in the

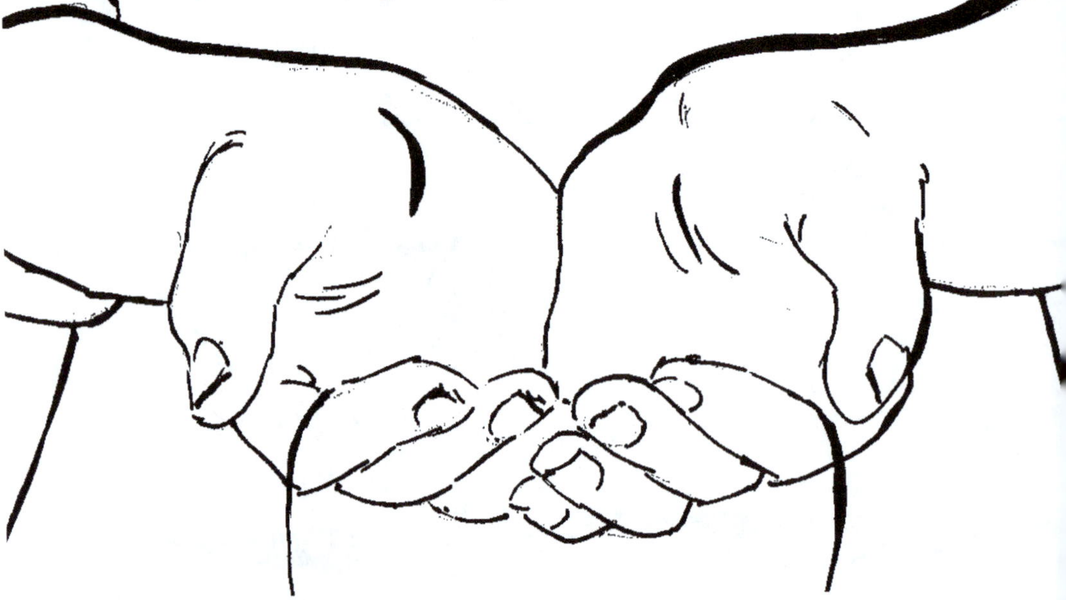

morning, meet in the late afternoon, lounge by the pool, and then have dinner at the Outback Steakhouse. I was drained by noon. I made use of the morning by scheduling an appointment with a COVID-19 laboratory and artist and got lost finding Copito Print. A woman in the waiting area noticed that I was struggling with a translator app and decided to help me. It never gets old to have someone speak English in Rio. My gratitude for her help was appreciated.

LAY OF THE LAND

INTRODUCTION TO ILLUSTRATOR

ADHEMAS BATISTA | Designer

Adhemas Batista started a career at age fifteen as a web designer. Throughout the years, he developed a distinctive visual style that has earned frequent press coverage and recognition in the highest ranks of the industry, including a Grand Prix for Good in 2016 for the short animation "Malak and the Boat" to raise awareness around the Syrian refugee crisis.

Adhemas has led and built design teams and co-founded a digital agency in Brazil and Los Angeles, California. Over the years, she's been lucky enough to work with most Fortune 500 brands, give lectures at workshops worldwide, and be featured at art galleries. Today she is the EVP at Deutsch Los Angeles, leading a team of 20 or more designers.

FIG 9-1

ASSESSMENT

Make the design connection. Answer the nourisher's and discuss them.

1. True or False: Anderson and Juliana agreed to take the day off, hang out, and relax. (Choose one)

- True
- False

2. What was the most striking aspect of the homeless man that Anderson saw? Choose the correct answer(s).

☐ His hair	☐ His toenails
☐ His age	☐ His fingernails

3. Meeting people in different circumstances can change one's outlook on life and motivate oneself to do better by his fellow man. (Choose one)

- Strongly agree
- Agree
- Neutral
- Disagree
- Strongly disagree

4. The chapter opens with a paragraph about a person struggling to reach a cross pendant. Why is this scene important, and how does it appear in the chapter later? (Discuss)

FIG 9-2

THE CHALLENGE | Lay of the Land

Lecture:

Students need to follow along to better understand the various tools used to create information on **Vector images, making the Grids**. The various types of grids would be covered in this lecture. Notes will be graded. Students will be asked to print samples and submit notes on the subject covered.

Scope:

The project is an animation about a favorite video from the Internet. Use design techniques and collected and/or written copy to depict a funny situation or joke. Information from the class exercise and textbook may be helpful. Use graph paper to research and plan out the strategy.

Begin drawing icons exercise in Illustrator.

Specifications:

File Size: 8.5 × 11in.
Art-board: Single-sided
File Type: .Ai
Design for: Print / Web
Fished File: Save as a .pdf file.
Submitting: Suitcase folder (L.Name-F.Name-ProjectName)

Hot Keyboard Shortcuts: Illustrator

CHAPTER 10
Lunch with Lucas

THE IDEA IN BRIEF | Adobe Illustrator

Intro to the *Pen* tool, *Transforming, Aligning,* using *Direct Selection* and *Anchor Points,* distorting *Shapes,* understanding *Paths, Stroke,* and *Fill* options. *File > Place* command. Working between Adobe Photoshop and Adobe Illustrator and the differences between them. Using images in Adobe Illustrator, *Live Trace,* and *Live Paint, Filters, Effects* and *Blends,* the *Libraries, Swatches,* creating *Pattern Swatches,* saving and using *Swatches.* Review on scanning photographs.

- **Concept Lecture:** The *type design* approach to solving challenges. A deeper look into *glyphs* and designing in other languages. Nine graphic styles.

Well-rested this morning, my workout was more invigorating. My body felt lighter and more limbo and lucid than a week ago. The vitamin regimen and the food here seem to work well. This time I got to see a little more of the beach. People are out moving about around 7:00 to 8:00 AM. The appearance of the athletic people of Copacabana, Rio, will keep you motivated to stay healthy, and there are many of them here. I walked a half-hour north on the boardwalk, almost halfway through. On the way, I used the workout stations and noticed a volleyball on a mole-hill-size pile of sand and empty Valley Court. On the way back, I recalled the large yellow tents and knew the hotel's street was near. There was also a seafood restaurant facing the beach on the same block, which made it a lot easier to recognize as well.

My room maid usually makes her rounds to the room around 10:00 AM. It's enough time to shower, eat breakfast, and meet Lucas, the interpreter. My room was on the fourth floor, the last junior suite facing the street intersection. When I returned to my room, I noticed that the maid didn't make the bed or cleaned it at this point. The weird thing was that the safe was open. I quickly kneeled over and reached to see if everything was still there. Thank God, nothing was missing. Baffled to find the safe open, I guessed there may be a malfunction.

After making it to continental breakfast, Lucas walked in heavily breathing and sweating while I was reporting the issue about the safe malfunction to the manager. He must have walked to the hotel from home. "Hey, Dyshann! How are you?" Management was taken a back by the greetings, so I introduced them to help make sense of why he was there. The staff at this point knew that I was a

foreigner and knew very little about why I was visiting Rio. Lucas stood behind me, fanning his sweaty Hawaiian print shirt by tugging it rapidly. He was waiting for me anxiously to end the conversation with the manager so we could start our meeting. "This is my interpreter, Lucas, and we are collaborating on a book project." After thanking the manager for help, I offered Lucas to sit in the lobby to explain this morning's incident with the safe.

Lucas and I sat in the lobby and spoke for hours. Our correspondence has been happening for weeks. We're trying to understand what we were to do for the book. Conducting interviews and transcribing was the task, and I thought his help was greatly appreciated. The simple plan was to search and interview. Lucas was recommended to me by another Portuguese translator from the United States—an older woman named Marcia. They both met while she was working for the consulate of the state of Rio. Marcia now lives in California but hasn't been to Rio for some time. She also mentioned Lucas was a second-generation interpreter who inherited the business from his mother.

Lucas's conversation was getting very political. The valet who spoke English was eavesdropping on the exchange. When I noticed, I kept diverting my questions off topic and trying to lead our discussion. After an hour of chatting and catching up, I invited him to lunch. Lucas knew the area and introduced me to a high-end restaurant named Ceasar Lanches three blocks from the hotel.

Last night I spoke to Juliana about meeting Lucas, and she warned me about the bandits. Lucas alluded to the women I knew in Rio, but I gave him a vague answer and brushed it off. Márca knows more about her but very little. For her protection, I shared very little of Juliana with anyone I knew there, and I didn't want her to be involved or plotted against because she was a friend.

Lucas shared a lot of personal information, but I stayed neutral in my responses and asked him logical questions to put things back into perspective. His comments about the government's decision to shut down a health facility full of people with mental health issues were thought provoking. "Hundreds of people lost from the facility are in the street and homeless," he expressed. I stood in

silence for a few minutes before telling him about my experience with the teenage girl on the beach early yesterday morning. Lucas's eyes whelped before I could finish, and tears started pouring from his eyes. When he realized he was crying, he used a linen cloth to wipe his face and change the conversation. Lucas is presently importing CBD products from Nevada, and he claims the product may be approved for doctors to prescribe. He testified that the product is reputable because it helped him with gingivitis.

The Ceasar Lanches's food was excellent, and the drinks were refreshing. We had caipirinhas, a famous lime in Brazil. The chilled pulp from the squeezed lime was refreshing. While enjoying the drinks, Lucas's wife called. "Hi honey, we're still here having lunch," Lucas said to his wife. He held the phone above his head and reversed the camera view to me on FaceTime, and she waved. I waved back and said, "Oi." The remaining afternoon was lighthearted, and we made lots of jokes. A laid out in a full spread of food with several plates, it was more than we could finish. After eating, I decided to take the leftovers back to the hotel. The waiter was great, Lucas grabbed the leftovers, and I paid for lunch. On the way back to the hotel, a homeless man asked us a question. Maybe about the food I thought; Lucas said, "Não" and kept walking. To my surprise, I looked at him strangely and suggested giving him the food, and he reluctantly obliged.

Communicating with the artist that night was successful, but I wanted to celebrate how well things were going so far. Juliana and I went to a hidden bar named Demi Copa, a small establishment North of Rio, which was quiet and chick. We had wine and coxinha pastry.

FONTS, HAND-LETTERING, AND TYPOGRAPHY

KIKO FARKAS | Designer, Illustrator

Kiko Farkas is a designer and illustrator. After graduating from the Faculty of Architecture of the University of São Paulo, Kiko works mainly in the editorial, cultural and institutional areas. He has directed Máquina Estúdio since its foundation in 1987. During this period, the Máquina Estúdio created outstanding projects such as MarcaBrasil, a visual identity for the Brazilian Tourism sector, the series of posters for Osesp—Orquestra Sinfônica do Estado de São Paulo and for Theatro Municipal de São Paulo. Currently, Kiko is devoted to developing and implementing teaching projects in visual communication, focusing on hybrid narratives among cinema, web, exhibition projects, and print media.

FIG 10-1

ASSESSMENT

Make the design connection. Answer the nourisher's and discuss them.

1. True or False: Lucas is an Brazilian futebal player. (Choose one)

- True
- False

2. Anderson and Lucas were collaborating on what kind of project? Choose the correct answer(s).

☐ A song ☐ A business

☐ A book ☐ A logo

3. You should avoid giving personal information to business partners/co-workers. (Choose one)

- Strongly agree
- Agree
- Neutral
- Disagree
- Strongly disagree

4. What impact does Anderson's meeting with the teenager have on the interpreter and others? (Discuss)

FIG 10-2

THE CHALLENGE | Fonts, Hand-lettering, and Typography

Design Brief

Students need to design **an Infographic Poster**. The lecture will cover *type design*. Collecting information will also be briefly covered and used throughout the poster. It's expected for students to take notes on the lessons covered in class and the textbook. Find the tools covered in the syllabus.

Scope:

The **Infographic Poster** project is a poster about a favorite fruit or vegetable. Use design techniques and collected copy to explain its health benefits. Information from the ***Lecture*** may be helpful. Use graph paper to research and plan out the strategy.

Specifications:

File Size: 17 × 11in.

Art-board: Single-sided

File Type: .Ai

Design for: Print

Fished File: Save as a .pdf file.

Submitting: Suitcase folder (L.Name-F.Name-ProjectName)

CHAPTER 11
Choices

THE IDEA IN BRIEF | Adobe Illustrator

Discover *Blends*, *Effects*, and *Distort;* they go unnoticed but highly effective in Adobe Illustrator. Master the *Pathfinder* panel. Drawing *Shapes* in Illustrator and the *Shape Builder* tool, *Blob Brush* tool, *Eraser* tool, *Pencil, Line* tool, and *Arc* tool. More drawing tools and a review *Shapes, Fill* and *Stroke*, arranging (stacking order) and *Layers. Selecting, Moving,* and *Aligning* objects. The function of tools dialog boxes that define the parameters of shapes.

- **Concept Lecture:** Graph pad review, and creating *First Draft, 2nd Draft,* and *Final Draft.* Brand scape and brand guidelines.

Sprinting down the beach's jogging lane, I can't believe I have the energy to move this fast. My body feels a lot stronger. This time I walked an hour out and another hour back. All I can think about is fruit for breakfast. I walked into the hotel, headed to the cafeteria, and saw Juliana waiting. She was holding a plastic bowl filled with fruit, and stopped eating. "I've been waiting for you a while. I'm charging my phone." I said, "Really,—no work today, huh?" "I'm working on-line today," she replied, then forked a slice of papaya and pineapple and slowly placed it into her mouth. I smiled and laughed out loud. I kindly explained that I must shower and work on my book. "I did my first interview yesterday and must transcribe my notes." She said, "You can do it in the pool area; I'll meet you there." That was reasonable, I thought to myself. I'm open to it. "Sure," I said unconvincingly.

My balance act had its corks with the expectation of a perfect work day. Before spreading my clothes for the day, I noticed there was very little to choose from in the primary suitcase. I didn't expect to shower twice in the days here in Rio, but it made sense in the hot weather and visiting restaurants and bars in the evening. The laundromat was convenient across the street from the Rio Design Hotel. The woman working in the laundromat accounts for the afternoon arrival of the clothes—"Great!" With my books and laptop in hand, I rode the elevator to the top level and saw Juliana in a bathing suit. She said "OK, ready to go?" Reflecting on the time, I thought I needed to make the deadline for my workbook, so my focus was work, work, work. The sun was beaming brighter on my cap brow every second, and the clear and blue sky didn't have a cloud in sight; t was surreal..

Time after time, minor interruptions break my focus. I compromised with Juliana to hang out on a full-day tour on Saturday. I needed to get work

completed. The inbox from the business was filling up and needed dire attention. An hour later, people from the hotel began to gather around the pool, playing music, laughing, and enjoying themselves. Before I can concentrate, the owner's wife from the hotel shows up with a clean supervisor, and the supervisor unplugs my laptop from behind the bar. Two minutes later, Juliana said, "I'm hungry, let's get lunch." My college professor often used to say, "Don't get distracted." Now I know what he meant by "distraction."

"OK, after lunch, I have to get to work," I said with a stern voice, "We can meet early this evening. It's Wednesday, and there's a lot to do." Separating business and socializing with Juliana will be challenging, but she has been great the whole trip. I'm a little worried about how to address the situation now, having to be diplomatic. She's an aggressive business owner and used to getting her way. It's either her or the book project.

Juliana picked up items off the deck, and we proceeded to a tourist eatery down the block that faced the beach. The restaurant has an open patio

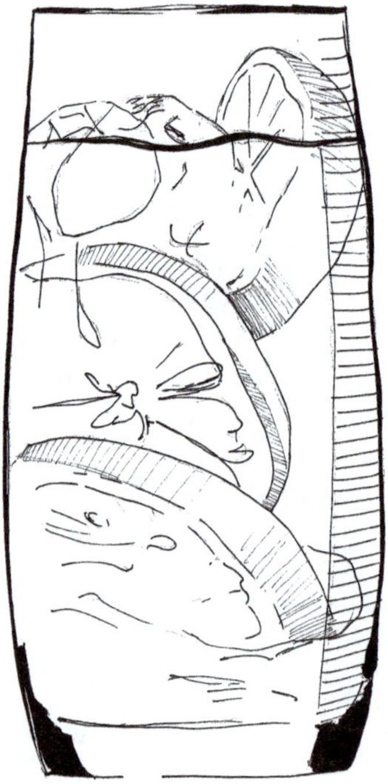

seating under a massive tent. We found a seat and ordered nonalcoholic drinks. A little tangled and agitated, I was able to loosen up since the pool fiasco. I checked my cell phone; 11:38 AM—it's almost noon, and I haven't accomplished much. Why not just relax and enjoy the sun for a moment. Juliana asked, "Are you OK?" "I'm fine. I guess food is good," I quickly responded. While the waiter served the drinks, chorões with a guitar and bongos moved leisurely on the patio and played. The waiter brought Juliana's food, and she began to eat while I watched curiously. The chorões musicians finished their set, and so was Juliana. She dropped her metal utensils onto the glass plate and dabbed her mouth off with a linen napkin. I was livid. My food still hasn't come yet. I asked Juliana to find out what was happening with the food. She corresponded with the waiter and said , "Wait a minute." I waited five minutes, then got up and handed the waiter money for the meal. He refused to take the payment, then surprisingly spoke English and said, “Wait a minute,” the waiter spoke in perfect english. I walked to my table annoyed, placed the money underneath my glass, and returned to my room.

A soggy veggie burger is what I had for dinner later on that night.

BRAND DESIGN, AND LOGOS

FRED GELLI | Co-founder, Creative Director

Fred Gelli is the co-founder and creative director of Tátil. This strategic consultancy uses design to create sustainable connections between people and brands, such as Coca-Cola, P&G, Philips, and TIM. Over his 27-year career trajectory, Gelli has accumulated over 100 national and international awards, including the iF Design Award, IDEA—USA, D&AD, and Cannes Lions. Recently, Gelli designed the Rio 2016™ Olympic and Paralympic Games Brands and served as the 2016 creative director of the Paralympic opening and closing ceremonies in Rio.

In 2014, Gelli was included in Fast Company's ranking of the 100 Most Creative People in the World, and his company was included in the Top 10 Most Innovative in South America. Fred has been a university professor in ecodesign and biomimicry at the Pontifical Catholic University of Rio de Janeiro.

FIG 11-1

ASSESSMENT

Make the design connection. Answer the nourisher's and discuss them.

1. True or False: Anderson and Juliana met at the pool area to work on a new website for a clothing line. (Choose one)

- True
- False

2. What did Dyshann bring with him to focus on work? Choose the correct answer(s).

☐ Laptop and book

☐ Laptop and pencil

☐ Notebook and pencil

☐ Book and notebook

3. It's crucial to separate business and socialization between co-workers. (Choose one)

- Strongly agree
- Agree
- Neutral
- Disagree
- Strongly disagree

4. Why do you believe that the chapter is named "Choices"?— How can choices determine self-identity and perception? (Discuss)

FIG 11-2

THE CHALLENGE | Brand Design—Logos

Design Brief

Students need to design a **personal logo** in Adobe Illustrator. Today's exercises are to design various symbols. It's expected for students to use the techniques covered in the class lecture and lessons in the textbook. Find the tools covered in the syllabus. Print the exercise and submit notes from the lecture.

Scope:

The logo project is a symbol that represents you personally to later use on resumes and self-promotional assets. Some ideas, maybe your favorite things, a letter-type, or an animal.—Never be afraid to explore the options. Information from Classroom In A Book, Chapters 1-4 may be helpful to review. Use graph paper to research and plan out the strategy. Create three options, pick one—then draw three more from the one you chose. Pick another—then draw three more. From the last three options, Choose one for your final to render in the Adobe Illustrator software.

Specifications:

File Size: 8.5 × 11in.
Color(s): B/W
Art-board: Single-sided
File Type: .Ai
Design for: Print
Fished File: Save as a .pdf file.
Submitting: Suitcase folder (L.Name-F.Name-ProjectName)

CHAPTER 12
Surprise, Surprise

THE IDEA IN BRIEF | Adobe Illustrator

Clipping Masks, more on *Filters, Blends, Objects* vs. *Type*, the use of *Layers* in Adobe Illustrator in comparison with Adobe Photoshop. Review the *Pen* tool and *Arranging (stacking order)* vs. *Layers.*

- **Concept Lecture:** *Gradients*, using *design elements* and *patterns* and the *psychology* that motivates design.

Early sleep gave me an early rise to work and completed a momentous day. After a cool shower and brushing my teeth, I noticed the enamel was returning to normal again. Comfortable clothes will bring less fatigue when walking in the city. Downtown Lapa, Rio was the destination by way of a taxi cab. A design school there caught my interest: InESDI—Incubadora de Empresas de Design Da ESDI (Industrial Design College and InESDI—ESDI Design Business Incubator). The college campus looked attractive on-line, and I wanted to look closer. Networking with the professors at the school will be invigorating. Sharing stories and experiences would be refreshing and maybe a way to gain insight into the art scene in Rio de Janeiro. If nothing goes my way, I'll visit the enormous mural of human history, which is located a few blocks away. It took a few minutes to gather my materials and COVID-19 information.

The process of getting to Lapa was a bumpy but smooth transition. The warm breeze was sticky and thick due to the rainfall I anticipate later this afternoon, so getting into air-conditioning was ideal. When I arrived with very little traffic in sight, the driver assured me that I was in the right location after my doubtful questioning. The address numbers of the building weren't visible right away. I thanked the driver with a smile and trusted him. I was only here to visit the sights and take in the art. The streets were clean, with people bustling around arriving to work. In Lopa, not one person wore sandals or flip-flops, which explained much about Copacabana. Copa is more for tourists and vacationers; this is where business happens here in Lopa, and I am anxious to get started. I walked further down the street curiously and noticed a couple of exciting restaurants down a side street—noted to me to have lunch there after the meeting. I approached security guards standing outside of the open corridor of the government building to ask them for directions. My translator app came into use when I texted an inquiry about the school address for the guards. I showed them my phone and said, "Please direct me to the school," in broken Portuguese. The taller guard pointed behind me and said, "Dessa maneira." The gate was closed, and I didn't notice the gates were covered with trees and overgrown shrubs upon arrival. I retraced my steps and met another pair of security guards standing at the entrance of a unique courtyard. The male and female guards were loftier. Their lax body language was welcoming, making me comfortable asking them probing questions.

I attempted to speak to school security guards in broken Portuguese and failed miserably, so I gave up and started speaking English. "Oh, Americano? " "Sim," I responded.

The female guard said "Gracia," to me and handed my phone back to me. The gentleman said, "Espere aqui, I'll find someone." After patiently waiting, I was approached by a stray cat. They were strays everywhere, walking freely around the public art sculptures in the courtyard. The landscapers also worked around me with clippers. One of them looked courteously at me for a second and said hello. Of course, I responded with a smile. The guard returns with João. He's a student-aid and specialized wood artisan. I showed him my employee ID, and he responded, "That's not necessary." "Thank you for taking the time out of your day to have this conversation; I'm an educator here to introduce myself and work." João talked and shared his work experiences. João was eager to show me around, and I was thankful and easily impressed by the campus and his explanation of the school curriculum. The tour led me to discussions about business and, of course, politics. Artists have celebrated Rio as they are in the United States but aren't supported as they should be in both countries, and we both agreed. I spent the morning trying to convince João that there was a market for the artist, but the challenge was finding the buyers.

After chatting in the morning, we then decided to have lunch. The narrow street of restaurants I saw earlier was João's usual scene. Since my visit to Rio, João introduced me to an attractive restaurant but a completely different operation than I have been. Restaurante Gutas restaurant was an all-you-can-eat what locals called a kilo restaurant. Everything was so fresh and flavorful.

João is very informed about the state's architectural history, and I felt he could have been a tour guide. He pointed out a few locations for me to visit for the afternoon. We parted ways at the electric transit system that ran through the city of Lapa. His assistant was going to deliver hand-made wooden bread cutters later, so we stayed in contact. Mural das Etnies, the enormous Graffiti in the World, was only a 5-minute train ride. After admiring the artwork, I walked down Pier Mauá and stopped in the Museu do Amanhã. Lucas texted me that afternoon. He wanted me to visit his home later in the afternoon, and I agreed. Juliana was still upset and wanted to get my mind off things quickly, so the timing was right. I assume he tried to introduce his wife and talk in detail about

the business. The showers stopped, and the sun was peeking through the clouds. The humidity was a little suffocating, so I found the nearest taxi stand and headed back to the hotel.

Lucas's house wasn't too far, but I was debating on a ride back to the hotel because of the rain. The sky was swelling up with clouds. After Lucas's stories about Americans visiting and doing bad things like wrongfully taking photos of women and selling them in the Japanese market was a guilt trip, so I decided to go anyway. I may sound melodramatic when I say Rio might be behind on spreading wealth among the Brazilian people. Still, they're light years ahead of building race relations and politics than the United States. The people of Rio de Janeiro t appeared to have a good understanding of one another, support, and get along well.

A bottle from the local super and deli should smooth things over, I thought to myself. Before I headed to Lucas's home, I picked up a bottle of Cachaça. During the cab ride, the clouds settled in, and it started pouring. Lightning lit up the sky behind the tall apartment buildings and exposed the favelas in the mountains. Lucas lived in a middle-class neighborhood in Leblon, a much more quaint location than Copacabana. Leblon Rio de Janeiro is two towns over from Copacabana just after Ipanema. The town isn't as lively as Copacabana. It reminded me a lot of home. I thanked the cab driver and waited in my raincoat for Lucas at the front of his eight-foot fenced condo complex. Lucas and I talked about the information collected and the CBD business for an hour until his wife walked in from work. She said, "Hello," and walked into a room down the hallway. A young woman came out of another room and into the kitchen five minutes later, opened a utensil drawer and the refrigerator door, and walked back down the hallway with a pint of ice cream in hand. Lucas didn't need to introduce her, and they never made eye contact which I thought was odd. My intuitions were on alert. Ten minutes later, Lucas friend arrived. I'd like to call him 'the professor' because he's an educator at a local college. Marijuana was his favorite subject matter. He was a skinny, brown-skin guy with round glasses. Minutes later, another friend barged in. His first words were, "Who is this?" I looked at him and sat there. This guy looks like Sylvester Stallone with a flushed red face but much droopier. Lucas invited me to hang out in the courtyard. The rain had slowed; we all stood underneath the garage ledge to prevent getting wet. Stallone offered to smoke marijuana, but I diplomatically declined and said, "No thanks, you can enjoy it." Again, Stallone started becoming a little aggressive and started speaking in Portuguese. I didn't understand what he said, but he seemed bothered for some reason. We returned to the house after a short time, and I alluded to leaving.

We were all standing between the kitchen and the living room. I was conversing with Lucas about the artist for the book, and all of a sudden, Stallone's, standing to my left, lifted his arms and gestured his fingers into guns pointed at me. All I could think about was getting out of Rio and arriving safely to my daughters.

My shoulders were squared toward Lucas. I took a half step backward with my left foot and folded my hand slowly together. My head was tilted towards Stallone, and I stared at him with fiery eyes. While walking around in his soul, he stood there silently when he realized that his day would worsen. I'm sure he got the message and knew it wouldn't end well. If one finger touched me, it would set off my survival mode. All I could think about was getting back to my daughters, and I was determined to leave if things got out of hand. During my visit to Lapa, I noticed the shipyard of freight boats; that's where I was headed if I wanted to leave the country. A couple of days ago, I ran a mile. My trainer decided to test me before I left for Brazil with the pads and gloves, and I almost dislocated his arms. These guys were out of shape, so I knew they didn't have a chance.

Lucas sent a convincing gesture to Stallone to relax, and I could walk out peacefully. I spoke to Lucas a few times after that incident, but I knew I would find an alternative interpreter for my book.

DIGITAL PORTRAITS, OR ANIMALS

UNIVERSO ACME | Artist, Entrepreneur

Acme has carried out works in several countries and states of Brazil; his art is part of the permanent collection of the National Historical Museum, Folklore Museum, and Favela Museum (RJ), in which he is a founding partner, creator, and curator of the Circuito das Casas-Tela, composer of Cordel and rap for MUF.

Main exhibitions include: Casino Atlântico—RJ, Cultural Center, Châteauvallon—Toulon, 2nd place at EUROGRAFF—Paris, by the HIP HOP Generation of SESC RJ (2005), International Art Meeting in Argentina, Art Paris, Grand Palais Galeria Adler Paris (France), Galpão das Artes in Rio Centro, Boulevard Olímpico (RJ), MuBE—Brazilian Museum of Sculpture (SP), Museum of Modern Art (RJ), Favela Museum, Museum National History (RJ), Folklore Museum (RJ), and Universidad Ray Juan Carlos in Madrid, Spain.

FIG 12-1

ASSESSMENT

Make the design connection. Answer the nourisher's and discuss them.

1. True or False: Anderson went to Downtown Lapa to visit a buffet. (Choose one)

- True
- False

2. What shoe did the people in Lopa NOT wear, according to Anderson? Choose the correct answer(s).

☐ Boots

☐ Adidas

☐ Sneakers

☐ Sandals/flip-flops

3. Maintaining a good relationship with associates or coworkers can impact the outcome of a project. (Choose one)

- Strongly agree
- Agree
- Neutral
- Disagree
- Strongly disagree

4. How did tensions rise during Anderson's meeting with Lucas and his friends?—How would you handle aggression to keep the peace among colleagues? (Discuss)

FIG 12-2

THE CHALLENGE | Portrait or Animal

Design Brief

Students need to design an **animal** or **self-portrait** from a photograph. Samples and a demo will be shown during the lecture. Graph paper is not needed for planning for this project, but research must be completed for color scheme and imagery then documented on graph paper instead. It's expected for students to use the lessons covered in class lectures and in the textbook.

Scope:

Use design techniques and the pen tool. Information from the symbol exercise may be helpful. Use good composition to display the subject and use past techniques to beautify the layout, patterns, textures, shapes, colors, grid, and type design.

Specifications:

File Size: 8.5 × 11in.
Art-board: Single-sided
File Type: .Ai
Design for: Print
Fished File: Save as a .pdf file.
Submitting: Suitcase folder (L.Name-F.Name-ProjectName)

CHAPTER 13
Day of Redemption

THE IDEA IN BRIEF | Adobe Illustrator

Review Illustrator tools, techniques, type, and typography. *Character* and *Paragraph* panel. Use of the *Grid* and *Guidelines* view for precision and control.

- **Concept Lecture:** Exploring today's design styles. 01. “Modern” Retro Style, 02. Material Design, 03. Bright, Bold Colors, 04. Geometric Shapes, 05. Negative Space, 06. Modular Layouts, 07. Dramatic Typography, 08. Custom Illustrations, 09. Abstract, Minimalistic Style. The Grids, Hey R.U.B.E.

My appointment at the laboratory for my COVID-19 test before my flight was at 7:30 AM. The previous visit made it easier to find. This time around, I took public transportation and made it there on time. The administrators made the process effortless. The results will be delivered over the weekend and ready for Monday, explained one young attendant. After visiting the COVID-19 laboratory, I decided to head to the cigar shop. The same cashier was there, and I remembered our conversation last weekend. I asked him about CAO Cigars and he didn’t recall. My guess was that it's just a brand dedicated to Brazil. The cashier gave me a short history lesson on authentic local cigars growers and handed me a few. I decided to walk back to the hotel to window shop and grab a glimpse of the street life.

Juliana called and invited me to the gym and meet at 10 o'clock. The gym was a five-minute walk past the grocery store, two blocks away. We made amends during the gym walk and realized it was a misunderstanding. Access was admitted to me in the gym with my COVID-19 card and digital fingerprint. This particular gym had two levels—Cardio on the first and free weights on the upper level. The gym equipment layout was packed, unlike most gyms in the United States. The free weights were in kilograms, so it made a little complicated, but I figured it out and understood that it was roughly half compared with pounds. The gym attendant carried a mini iPad and was friendly, but he couldn't speak English, so I had to revert to my translator. I was okay on my own; I've been working out since high school, and I played college football, so I knew how to get around in the gym. The attendant was helpful when alternating the equipment with other members. While I was working out, the attendant approached me with another guy, about five-seven, dressed

in a red-and-white Nike jumpsuit. The attendant explained to him I was from the United States and introduced us. It was a heavy day, so I reduced the weight before he began his set. He readjusted it back and was able to complete the reps. The second time around, he struggled. Eventually, I finished my reps and moved to the another machine. Twenty-minute workouts and an hour of cardio are usually what my day looks like on average during stay in Rio.

After the gym, we went to Ferrell Postel 6 restaurant to have lunch. I believe Ferrell is a restaurant chain. The decor reminds me a lot of the United States. I've ordered food and desserts from this restaurant and had it delivered to Juliana in the past. One of the waitresses recognizes me from my Whats-app image. The restaurant is not too far from Juliana's home, so I assume she visits often and knows her well. While we were eating, every once in a while, I saw a new person peeking from the kitchen area, staring and smiling. I smiled and waved back at them. He, he!

Juliana and I split up and convene late that afternoon. A lot of my work was completed after the exercise and lunch, so I was open to doing whatever. I didn't

tell her what happened at Lucas's house, and I didn't want to concern her about it. Juliana goes to church on Friday nights. I invited myself to see the architecture and Brazilian people in their natural elements. They're very religious, which will give me a better understanding of the culture. Before heading to church, we stopped at a flower stand and grabbed two sunflowers. I don't understand the significance of the sunflowers, and I didn't ask. I assumed she often brings them as an offering. Along the way, she met a few people in the neighborhood and chatted with them. She introduced me, but I couldn't speak Portuguese fast enough so I kept it cordial.

The church was just across the street from Juliana's apartment building, down a hidden corridor that led to the beach. She took me through a small narrow door and walked down along the labyrinthine highway. We eventually got to the entrance of the cathedral with teenagers hanging out. Past the doors was a set of stairs illuminated by wood paneling. I followed Juliana and looked left. There were stage props and stadium-like seating of leather chairs in the cathedral. You couldn't tell from outside the building that a more extensive complex was inside. There were no windows, just stained glass sections with wood frames. The sermon was loud. The main prop was a slight triumphal arch. Juliana asked me to wait in my seat while she took the set and stood in line to pass through the arch and take communion. She danced and prayed for a full hour. The pastor was young and orchestrated the crowd with significant influence.

JESUS CR
O SENHOR

INFOGRAPHIC POSTER, BROCHURE, OR MENU

BEATRIZ FEITLER (February 5, 1938–April 8, 1982)
Graphic Designer

Beatriz (Bea) Feitler was a Brazilian graphic designer who worked for Harper's Bazaar, Ms., Rolling Stone, and several other magazines. She was the first art director to feature a black model in a major fashion magazine. Bea was also a key figure behind the relaunch of Vanity Fair in the early 1980s. She died of cancer slightly before the first issue was out of print, only 44 years old.

FIG 13-1

ASSESSMENT

Make the design connection. Answer the nourisher's and discuss them.

1. True or False: Juliana purchased two roses on the way to church. (Choose one)

- True
- False

2. What measurement units were the free weights in at the gym? Choose the correct answer(s).

☐ Pounds

☐ Kilograms

☐ Ounces

☐ Grams

3. Visiting culturally significant places can help one better understand the artistic design style and incorporate it into their projects. (Choose one)

- Strongly agree
- Agree
- Neutral
- Disagree
- Strongly disagree

4. How does attending a church service help Anderson understand Rio's culture and the layout of the architecture? (Discuss)

FIG 13-2

THE CHALLENGE | Self-promotion – Résumé

Design Brief

Students need to design **a new resume** with their **logo project**. Find a resume sample on-line. Use a graphic art ruler to decipher the measurements of your model. It's expected for students to use the lessons covered in class and the textbook. Find the topics covered in the syllabus and the book.

Scope:

The resume is a document that should highlight your history in the job market, experience, areas that you're skilled in, and education. Use design techniques and collected research to understand the structure better and discover the multiple grids ideas. Instruction from the ***class lecture*** **and Chapter 8 in your textbook** may be helpful. Use graph paper to research and plan out the strategy.

Specifications:

File Size: 8.5 × 11in.
Art-board: Single-sided
File Type: .Ai
Design for: Print
Fished File: Save as a .pdf file.
Submitting: Suitcase folder (L.Name-F.Name-ProjectName)

CHAPTER 14
Sugarloaf

THE IDEA IN BRIEF | Adobe Illustrator

Review Adobe Photoshop and Adobe Illustrator tools, techniques, and typography. Understanding types of Grids anatomy, print dialog box, and building in spell-checking habits.

- **Concept Lecture:** Using stock images, templates, and learning demographics, geographic, and behaviors of target markets. Copywriting and editing.

As promised, Juliana and I met in the morning for our tour of attractions. When I came down from my hotel room, she was already in the cafeteria eating fruit and potatoes stuffed with cheese. We had breakfast and chatted about the church sermon last night. Juliana randomly takes pictures of me, and I'm unsure what to make of it. I alluded to this because she said, "You're a beautiful American man. You're fortunate to have me." I responded, "We are lucky to have each other," and smiled at her. I'm not sure how she took it, but I feel we always need to be on the same playing field.

A tall guy entered the lobby with full of energy and noticed us waiting in the cafeteria. He knew who we were and was delighted to take us on tour. We got in a small 15-passenger Sprinter van. Our guide, Gustavo, introduced us to the driver, and we made our way throughout the city, picking up the rest of the tourists from different hotels. After our last pick-up, we headed to Christ the Redeemer. Gustavo wanted to avoid the crowd and rain. We had to drive through the favelas to get to the monument. The streets were very tight and narrow. The favelas were peaceful and non-threatening, contrary to popular belief. There was art throughout the entire drive there. Fifteen to twenty minutes into the tour, we approached a rest stop overlooking Rio. The site of Copacabana beach was so far in the distance, and the mist got thicker as we drove closer to the world-famous monument. Police officers were randomly posted along the way, and when we got there, they greeted us. The driver spoke in Portuguese, and the officer let us through. As a group, we headed into the gift shop to wait for a tour guide to give us tickets. After getting our tickets, we could take photographs and a couple of elevators to get there. After the two elevators and an escalator, we finally arrived to the Christ the Redeemer monument. It felt epic because I've only seen it in photos as a child. The tall white statue was humongous.

The sea mist cloaked the monument, and the tropical birds flying around were an unbelievable experience. Gustavo was right; after 10 minutes of taking photographs and videos, tourists swarmed the large monuments' platform. There were people from all over the world. As instructed, we were able to meet with Gustavo at the meeting location.

We visited three other sites before grabbing lunch. The second site was the carnival stadium. Gustavo said the city created the stadium pathway on the main street after many years. The performers complained about the distance and heat. The following location was the enormous Cathedral of St. Sebastian, an architectural feat with large glass windows. Juliana loved this location and decided to take a moment and pray for a few minutes. I was able to admire the façades and sculptures throughout the cathedral. After a few photographs, we moved on to the third location, the Escadaria Selaron, the iconic steps of Lapa. The steps were a work of art designed by an artist from Chile. This artist fell in love with a Brazilian woman and was bothered by walking broken steps, so he took it upon himself to plaster tiles on the stairway. These tiles had pictures of his love for his pregnant wife, tortured and burned for unknown reasons. Famous people like Pharrell Williams and Snoop Dogg have visited the steps to salute the couple and the child in a music video.

Surprisingly, the restaurant Gustavo chose was a typical kilo buffet restaurant. I was in the neighborhood on Thursday with João, the student aid Industrial

Design College. Me Gusta Gourmet Restaurante was on the same street and was a much larger establishment with various meats, salads, and desserts.

After stuffing ourselves at the restaurant, the tour continued to the last location, Sugarloaf Mountains, Pão de Açucar, also known as the Sugarloaf. The Sugarloaf is a natural phenomenon created by volcanic rock. Visitors travel on a ski lift or helicopter to and from the mainland and mountains. The Sugarloaf is a famous mountain and can be seen all over the city of Rio because of its size. There were gift shop directions and history about the Sugarloaf at the first mountain location. The group didn't have time to view everything on site, but we could see more on the second mountain. On this mountain, restaurants were hidden throughout the main area, a beautiful place over Guanabara Bay. Three hundred ninety-six meters above the harbor gave a new perspective to Copacabana and the rest of Rio. Being this high above land gave me new ideas about places to visit. The stores, small shops, and restaurants filled the rest of the day. Gustavo gave us the thank-you speech and headed back to the mainland, but we decided to stay and spend the rest of the day lounging at Pao de Acucar Gourmet. Around 4 o'clock, we agreed to head back to the hotel to get ready for dinner. On the way down, we could visit the gift shops and grab a few things; a Flamingo futebol jersey was a high priority. Today was excellent, and I decided to come back for another visit and see more of Rio.

INFOGRAPHIC POSTER
BROCHURE
MENU

ELAINE RAMOS | Graphic Artist

Brazilian designer Elaine Ramos studied architecture at the School of Architecture and Urbanism at the University of São Paulo (FAU-USP). Her work has included identity design, posters, album covers, curatorship (such as "Cidade gráfica," 2014), and exhibition design, including "Sertão" at the Museu de Arte Moderna (MAM) in 2019. However, her commitment has always been to editorial design, and over eleven years (2004—15), her design and art direction for Brazilian publishing house Cosac Naify attracted widespread acclaim, with books such as translations of Philip Meggs' *History of Graphic Design / História do design gráfico* (2012) and Samuel Beckett's *First Love / Primeiro Amor,* as well as a book about Brazilian musician João Gilberto. In 2015, Ramos cofounded the publishing house Ubu, which has continued where Cosac Naify left off.

FIG 14-1

ASSESSMENT

Make the design connection. Answer the nourisher's and discuss them.

1. True or False: Anderson and Juliana first visited the Christ the Redeemer statue during the tour due to inclement weather. (Choose one)

- True
- False

2. What pictures were included on the tiles of the Escadaria Salon? Choose the correct answer(s).

☐ The artist's favorite foods

☐ The artist's friends

☐ The artist's kids

☐ The artist's love for his pregnant wife

3. Touring famous places and relating to the stories is essential when visiting a new country. (Choose one)

- Strongly agree
- Agree
- Neutral
- Disagree
- Strongly disagree

4. Why do you believe that the author chose the location Sugarloaf in particular, for the chapter's name? (Discuss)

FIG 14-2

THE CHALLENGE | Infographic Poster, Brochure, or Menu

Design Brief

Students need to design a local business **brochure/take-out menu**. Use a graph research paper to plan out the strategy and layout. Download the template from https://www.gotprint.com/resources/templates/info.html > Brochure > 8.5x11 > Half Fold Horizontal > Ai. Students are expected to use the lessons covered in class and Chapter 5 in the textbook. Find the topics covered in the syllabus.

Scope:

The brochure project is for the student to update a **brochure/take-out menu**. Use design techniques and collected copy to explain its featured items and list of products. Retype the information and search the Internet for better images *(be mindful of the image sizes you're working with)*. If you need to modify the photos, please use Photoshop CC. Use graph paper to research and plan out the strategy.

Specifications:

File Size: 8.5 × 11in.
Art-board: Single-sided
File Type: .Ai
Design for: Print
Finished File: Save as a .pdf file.
Submitting: Suitcase folder (L.Name-F.Name-ProjectName)

CHAPTER 15
Last Night

THE IDEA IN BRIEF | Adobe Illustrator

At this point and time you should be familiar with Adobe Illustrator tools, techniques, and design methodologies to strategize the last two challenges. Archiving for multiple assets for design campaigns.

- **Concept Lecture:** The commercial printing process and visiting our neighborhood production house. *File Set-up* for deployment. Branding for *In-store (stationery) Product or Service*, and *Digital (social media).*

I don't know how something like that happens after a whole night's sleep. The tour has taken a toll on me. Juliana and I agreed to part ways after we returned to the hotel then parted ways. We were both exhausted last night. João's assistant has planned to meet to complete a purchase of hand-made bread cutters. Samara was an illustrator that lived in the neighborhood of my hotel. She told me there was a better park and beach not too far and agreed to show me around after her purchase. Juliana texted me she was in the café waiting for me. I mentioned the transaction on tour yesterday. She must have forgotten. After the business exchange and friendly conversation, I assured her of returning for lunch. Before walking Juliana home, we stopped to grab coffee at her favorite cafe. When I arrived back at the hotel, Samara was waiting at the lobby counter, speaking to the valet. João's hand-made bread knives were created from Redwood trees; it's a complete set stained and branded. The bread-cutting knives are beautiful, and I wish I could look forward to purchasing more of João's woodwork. João and I traded information to do more business later. There's a massive market in Connecticut for hand-made kitchen products.

Samara arrived at 10 AM and gave me a tour. We walked south of Ave. Nossa Sra de Copacabana, and she gave me a brief history of the neighborhood. A street market sprung up on Ave. Rainha Elisabeth, between Nossa Sra and Ave. Atlantica, with vendors selling indigenous fruits. It took about 10 minutes before we cut through a school playground. Halfway through, we walked past a ramp covered in shrubs. Samara warned me of this area, "There are crack-heads up there," she said. "Don't go up there." I quickly responded, "You know the term crack-heads," and laughed.

The parking lot opened up to a large space, and we eventually ended our short journey at a sandy beach. Samara said, "This beach is called Praia do

Arpoador!" The water was so apparently clearer than Copacabana beach. The complex sounds of children laughing song along the warm breeze. Crashing waves on the nearby rocks was grand massive. The beach is large in comparison to Copacabana. Samara went back and we decided to part ways. "Thank you so much for showing me around and a history lesson," I said with gratitude.

"There's very little time left to enjoy; I'd wish I knew it was a short walk away." "Well, you'll be back again, I'm sure. Have a safe trip back to the States." Samara shook my hand and waved goodbye.

On my way back, I stopped by the open street market and looked around. There was a lot of indigenous fruits I wanted to try, but I was unclear about my allergies, plus there were too many people waiting around. I got a text from Juliana, and I told her to meet me at the Mercardo Zonasul supermarket to grab something for us to eat. We had lunch, and I spent the remaining day packing for my trip tomorrow with two fewer outfits for tonight and tomorrow.

Juliana and I split up to get dressed, and she texted me when she arrived in the lobby downstairs. The night was clear with less humidity and no cloud in sight, and the warm wind pushed the scent of the sea between the tall buildings. We chose the first of many taxis at the stand and headed to the Bolada Mix, where we had our last dinner. His restaurant was superb with great energy. I enjoyed myself here, but the night didn't overwalk the beat, and I randomly chose Fafato Restaurant Bar e Pizzaria for a nightcap.

PRODUCTION DESIGN

CARTON BOX

ERICK ROOT | Furniture and Industrial Designer

Curiosity and creativity—two simple words with such significant meaning! Isn't it? The most straightforward way to tell how we got here today with the world around us is by explaining the curiosity that moves us to understand the world around us and the creativity to solve the problems that our interest finds on our path.

To use and harvest both of these aspects of being a human is the duty of any person who decides to work in the creative industry, and I took this as a way of life. Curious and creative.

FIG 15-1

ASSESSMENT

Make the design connection. Answer the nourisher's and discuss them.

1. True or False: João's handmade bread knives were created from redwood trees. (Choose one)

- True
- False

2. Where did Samara take Anderson during the short tour? Choose the correct answer(s).

☐ A famous resturant	☐ The beach
☐ Street market	☐ Surfing

3. Visiting a new location or restaurant each time is better than revisiting the same place in a different country/state. (Choose one)

- Strongly agree
- Agree
- Neutral
- Disagree
- Strongly disagree

4. How do the various details about the people and places the author encounters help readers visualize the story? (Discuss)

FIG 15-2

THE CHALLENGE | Package Design—Carton Box

Design Brief:

Students need to create a product design for the final project. A handout of the template will be provided to use with graph paper to plan out the strategy, size, design elements, color schemes, and layout. During the next two weeks, it's expected for students to use research and collect copy (content) and design for this project. Improvements will be graded on aesthetics because of the time allowed to create. Project reviews will be conducted during class as needed.

Scope:

The **Carton Box** project is an opportunity for **the designer to be innovative**. Use the projects to brand the product. Use elements of a milk carton to set a standard and use your imagination to recreate the remainder. **Please print the finished file in color**. Use the syllabus and project rubrics to refresh your memory about the specs.

Specifications:

File Size: Template provided.

Art-board: Single-sided

File Type: .Ai

Design for: Print

Finished File: Save as a .pdf file and print

Submitting: Suitcase folder (L.Name-F.Name-ProjectName)

CHAPTER 16
Say Goodbye

THE IDEA IN BRIEF | Adobe Illustrator

Planning and organization has been essential in proficiency as a graphic artist. Nothing can be more detrimental than a scattered brain in a complex design challenge. Distractions should be accounted for and discipline can keep a creative mind from going astray. Developing the Crook can take years to develop; trust in your intuition and instincts.

- **Concept Lecture:** Being a graphic artist in today's changing world and how to adapt.

The day started great. My clothes were packed, and breakfast was waiting for me. The room was cleared before wheeling my luggage to the elevator. Before I pressed the down-arrow button, I said to myself, "I will miss this place." Ding, the doors opened up and closed while I stared at the artwork on the hallway walls. While waiting for my travel documents to print, I had breakfast and said my goodbyes to all the friendly staff workers. Juliana decided to bid me farewell and accompany me to breakfast and to the airport. My escort from Booking.com arrived at 11 am precisely, and to Juliana's surprise, the driver was in his car. It was a younger gentleman, very polite, and was eager to get me from the hotel to the airport on time. The driver wasn't aware that my flight was at 11:55

PM. We arrived early to avoid the traffic and the crowds, but I didn't know what to expect from the airport. I've only been here once before. While waiting patiently for the Delta's terminal to open, Juliana and I discussed business plans. The work never ends.

While waiting for the terminal to open for check-in, Juliana and I waited patiently and listened to the rain pour heavily on the corrugated metal above the airport ceiling. One after another, the Delta attendance was slowly preparing for passenger traffic. I casually walked up to an attendant with my bags and said "Oi," then to the check-in while Juliana stayed seated texting on her cell phone. I couldn't check-in at the kiosk, so I approached the second attendant, and he asked me, "How was your stay? Did you enjoy Rio?" "I responded enthusiastically, "Very well, there's so much to see and very little time!" I handed the attendant my ticket, ID passport, and COVID-19 results. The attendant looked at my documents for several seconds and paused, then raised his eyebrows. "I can't accept this," the attendant gradually replied. With a baffled expression on my face, I answered his response slowly, confused, and asked him, "Why not?" Juliana quickly shut her phone down and

approached the counter while the attendant tried to explain to me—"The results were outdated; you have to report within twenty-four hours. I took a step back and Juliana spoke to the gentleman in Portuguese, "O que está acontecendo com os documentos dele?" The attendant's posture retracted, and he explained again and more agitated, "O resultado tem que sair em 24 horas. Aqui diz que os resultados foram no sábado, agora é segunda-feira…" "I can't accept this," he said in English. I responded, "The labs were closed on the weekend, so can you get a test on Sunday to have it ready by Monday?" The attendant suggested that I get the COVID-19 test again at the airport. "The test usually takes a few hours," he said. "You may still have time to make your flight at 11:55 PM. But I'm not sure of their hours, and you must check downstairs on the lower level."

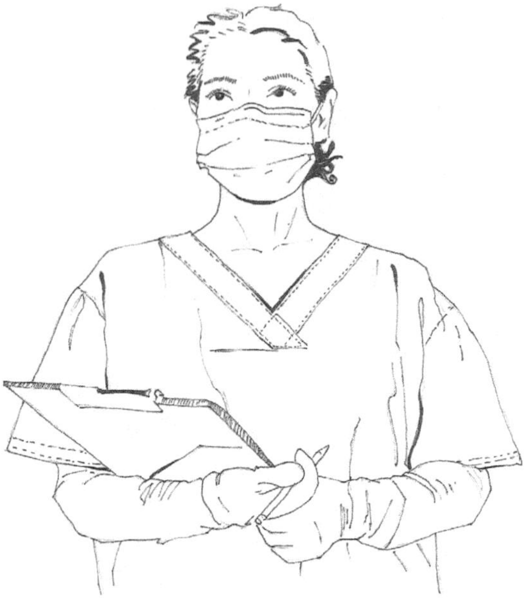

I walked away in shock, desperate, and unclear if I would make it home. Juliana tried to assure me that things were going to be okay. “Don’t worry. You can make it home.” We wheeled my luggage to the elevator, then downstairs to the lower level, and spoke to the lab assistant. Dressed in a lab coat and standing at a podium with a laptop, she spoke English and explained that I had to pay for the test before actually administering it. “What time is your flight?” The lab assistant asked. I anxiously responded quickly and said, “11:55.” "Hurry, you may still have time, depending on the lines.” Juliana agreed to stay with the luggage as I returned upstairs to purchase another COVID-19 test from Sociedade Benef Israeli. There was a small line with older people trying to make sense of the process and asking questions. I checked my cell phone every 5 minutes past 7:00 PM while the clerks dressed in matching gray uniforms were friendly and patient.

Needless to say, I did make my flight back home, but I did learn a lot about Brazil and what things to keep in mind while visiting another country.

ON
QC
NB
PE
NS
WI
MI
IL
IN
OH
PA
MD
DE
VA
NC
SC
MS
AL
GA
FL
North Atlantic Ocean
ulf of exico
Cuba
Puerto Rico
temala
Caribbean Sea
Nicaragua
Venezuela
Guyana
Suriname
Colombia
RR
AP
Ecuador
AM
PA
MA
CE
RN
PB
PI
PE
AL
SE
Brazil
AC
Peru
RO
TO
BA
MT
GO
Bolivia
MS
SP
Paraguay
PR
Chile
SC
RS
Uruguay

PRINT AND DIGITAL

BRAND CAMPAIGN

PAULO NAZARETH | Contemporary Artist

Paulo Nazareth was born in 1977 in Governador Valadares, Minas Gerais, Brazil, and is of Afro-Brazilian descent. Nazareth builds relationships with the diverse individuals he meets while traveling for his art—often long distances by foot—and these people encourage his works of art. In March 2011, Paulo walked from Minas Gerais, Brazil, to New York in the United States. This solo journey took him five months as Paulo traveled by foot thousands of miles north, never washing his bare feet, refraining only until he could pass them in eastern New York's Hudson River ritualistically. The trip served as a form of performance—he gauged the reactions of the people he interacted with as he passed through their towns and cities, receiving their feelings about himself, specifically his racial identity and appearance.

FIG 16-1

ASSESSMENT

Make the design connection. Answer the nourisher's and discuss them.

1. True or False: Anderson's flight out of Rio was at 9:45 PM. (Choose one)

- True
- False

2. What did Anderson purchase at the Sociedade Benef Israeli? Choose the correct answer(s).

☐ Back message

☐ Neck pillow

☐ COVID-19 test

☐ Beers and burgers

3. Was it necessary to visit another country to create this particular workbook? (Choose one)

- Strongly agree
- Agree
- Neutral
- Disagree
- Strongly disagree

4. How is Anderson's research trip to Rio compared with his trip to Miami in Chapter 5? (Discuss)

FIG 16-2

THE CHALLENGE | Brand Campaign

Design Brief/Scope:

Students need to design In-store Brand Campaign for a non-profit or business. Use graph paper to plan out the strategy and layout. The design assets created would be as follows: In-store (Ai); Event flyer (5 × 7in; Featured item poster (13 × 19in); Save the date bookmark (2 × 8in). Social Network (Ps); Social media cover photo (1773 × 656px), social post (472 × 394px), profile picture logo (180 × 180px), social media stop-motion gif (1920 × 1080px .gif). Students are expected to use the lectures covered in class and the lessons in the textbook. Use the Brands of the World website to download brand logos. Ensure you note "for educational purposes only" on all design assets. Research the topics covered in the syllabus.

Specifications: The brand project is a campaign about a featured product or service. Use design techniques and collected copy to explain its benefits. Information from past projects may be helpful. (Please submit projects in a digital suitcase. You are graded on the native, research, and finished files).

File Size: poster, flyer, social media, postcard 8.5 × 11in.
Color: CMYK, RGB
Art-board: Single-sided / double-sided
File Type: .Adobe Photoshop and Illustrator
Design for: Print and Web
Finished File: Save as .jpeg, .gif, ands .pdf file(s).
Submitting: Suitcase folder (L.Name-F.Name-ProjectName)

THANK YOU

Juliet Kimble

Gary Rhule, MD

Mr. Baylock

Maura O'Conner

Andy Fulp

Amy Kern

Dr. Thomas Zummer

Shutter Stock Photo Credits

1306022545 brandpunkt

1740444743 Kri haneth

1187515993 Sheila Fitzgerald

1816314965 Bruno Mar ns Imagens

331245566 Allyso

1552104335 SB Arts Media

712625887 Sean Pavone

1068097025 Bob Korn

1033133341 EQRoy

80947111 Mar n M303

1565941951 A.RICARDO

2007761879 Luis War

176322233 Catarina Belova

1383275822 Catarina Belova

1475846993 takepicsforfun

1515705980 lazyllama

1082174216 Catarina Belova

1492458569 Antonio Salaverry

1714681855 Cryptographer

Brazilian Graphic Design

Gallery Patricia Costa

Tramas Arte Contemporânea

Zeca Pagodinho

www.ingramcontent.com/pod-product-compliance
Lightning Source LLC
LaVergne TN
LVHW050819061126
851857LV00012B/877
* 9 7 9 8 7 6 5 7 4 3 1 4 0 *